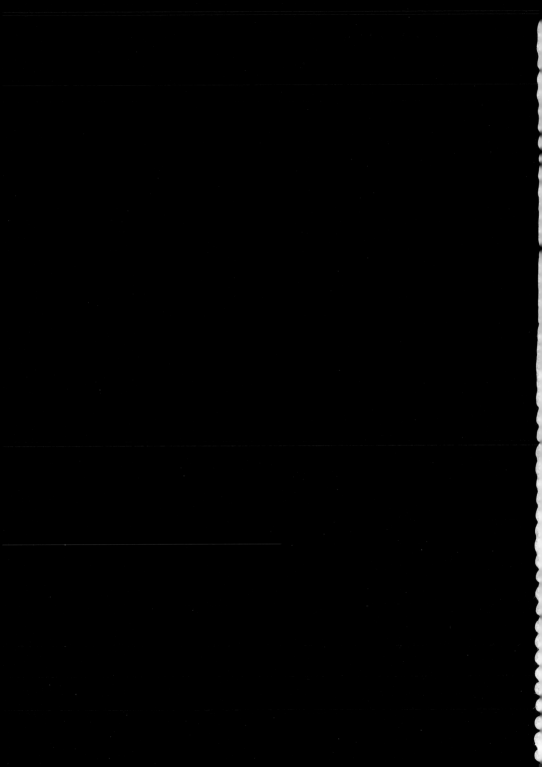

The Mocktail Club

CLASSIC RECIPES (AND NEW FAVORITES)
WITHOUT THE BOOZE

DERICK SANTIAGO

Adams Media

New York London Toronto Sydney New Delhi

Adams Media
An Imprint of Simon & Schuster, Inc.
100 Technology Center Drive
Stoughton, Massachusetts 02072

First Adams Media hardcover edition January 2024

ADAMS MEDIA and colophon are registered trademarks of Simon & Schuster, Inc.

Simon & Schuster: Celebrating 100 Years of Publishing in 2024

For information about special discounts for bulk purchases, please contact Simon & Schuster Special Sales at 1-866-506-1949 or business@simonandschuster.com.

The Simon & Schuster Speakers Bureau can bring authors to your live event. For more information or to book an event, contact the Simon & Schuster Speakers Bureau at 1-866-248-3049 or visit our website at www.simonspeakers.com.

Interior design by Colleen Cunningham
Photographs by Harper Point Photography
Interior illustrations © 123RF/Andrey Vinnikov; Getty Images/Tetiana Lazunova

Manufactured in the United States of America

10 9 8 7 6 5 4 3 2 1

Library of Congress Cataloging-in-Publication Data
Names: Santiago, Derick, author.
Title: The mocktail club / Derick Santiago.
Description: First Adams Media hardcover edition. | Stoughton, Massachusetts: Adams Media, 2024. | Includes index.
Identifiers: LCCN 2023037726 | ISBN 9781507221631 (hc) | ISBN 9781507221648 (ebook)
Subjects: LCSH: Non-alcoholic beverages. | Cocktails. | LCGFT: Cookbooks.
Classification: LCC TX815 .S267 2024 | DDC 641.87/5--dc23/eng/20230905
LC record available at https://lccn.loc.gov/2023037726

ISBN 978-1-5072-2163-1
ISBN 978-1-5072-2164-8 (ebook)

This book is not affiliated or associated with the beverage manufacturer Mocktail Club, which is well known for its popular line of prepackaged nonalcoholic cocktails.

To my mother, whose love for all things culinary
inspired my love for mixology.

CONTENTS

PART 1

MOCKTAILS 101 · 11

CHAPTER 1. WHAT ARE MOCKTAILS? · 12

PART 2

THE RECIPES · 35

CHAPTER 2. GIN-INSPIRED MOCKTAILS · 36

CHAPTER 3. RUM-INSPIRED MOCKTAILS · 53

CHAPTER 7. APERITIFS · 119

CHAPTER 8. SPIRIT-FREE MOCKTAILS · 137

ACKNOWLEDGMENTS

This book wouldn't have been possible without the support of my partner, Carlton; my siblings, Liann and Joshua; family members; and friends. Thank you to Eileen and the rest of the Adams Media team for the opportunity and support.

INTRODUCTION

Mocktails today are worlds apart from the mocktails of the past. Thanks to today's increasingly wide array of zero-proof and nonalcoholic spirits, beers, wines, and bitters, modern mocktails are breaking boundaries and changing minds! With substitutes for whiskey, rum, gin, and other spirits, now you can create quality nonalcoholic drinks that have the same complexity, appearance, and taste as standard cocktails—just without the alcohol.

The Mocktail Club offers seventy-five alcohol-free recipes that reflect the same care and attention to detail that one would invest in a craft cocktail. From plays on classic cocktails to new flavor concoctions, the options are endless. The creative mocktails in this book are all about fresh ingredients, classic flavors, and keeping the booze out, so you can bring the fun of a classic cocktail bar right to your couch.

Inside, you'll find recipes for:

- Lavender Lemon Drop Martini
- Mango Rum Cooler
- Watermelon Margarita
- Irish Coffee
- Cherry Vanilla Blush
- Strawberry Negroni Smash
- And more!

You'll also gain the knowledge and skills—such as learning about basic bar tools and glassware, simple mocktail making techniques like dry and wet shaking, and popular ingredients to have on hand—so that you can create elevated mocktails at home for yourself and for guests.

So, regardless of your reason for not consuming alcohol, you can still enjoy a carefully crafted adult drink with balanced, delicious, and complex flavors all served in a fancy glass with a beautiful garnish. This book will show you how.

PART 1

Mocktails 101

Before you can dive into the exciting world of making mocktails, you'll need a bit of background. In this first part, you will learn about the primary no- or low-alcohol spirit alternatives, how they are made, and their respective flavor profiles. You'll also learn the critical differences between spirits labeled "alcohol-free," "zero-proof," "nonalcoholic," and "dealcoholized" so you can make informed decisions when choosing between these options.

CHAPTER 1

WHAT ARE MOCKTAILS?

A mocktail is, by definition, simply a cocktail (mixed drink) without any alcoholic content. This absence of alcohol does not mean that mocktails are inferior. In fact, one often invests a lot of creativity and care in making mocktails that simulate the taste of cocktails. And that is one goal of this book: to help you create quality nonalcoholic drinks that are analogous, or even equivalent, to cocktails in terms of complexity, appearance, social cachet, and of course taste—just without the alcohol.

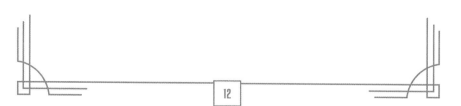

MOCKTAIL TERMINOLOGY

Perhaps because of unfamiliarity with the new alcohol alternatives, mocktails have suffered an undeserved bad reputation in some quarters. Some dismiss mocktails as being merely a combination of fruit juices, overly sweet, or just a kid's drink. Some also oppose the term "mocktail" altogether because of these negative connotations, or because they interpret the prefix "mock" to mean "mockery of a cocktail" rather than "a facsimile."

In place of the term "mocktail," many people use alternative descriptions like "nonalcoholic," "alcohol-free," or "zero-proof." Now, these terms are great, especially if they help make craft cocktails without the alcohol more mainstream. However, did you know that these terms have important differences among them?

Nonalcoholic, Alcohol-Free, Zero-Proof, or Dealcoholized

The terms "nonalcoholic," "alcohol-free," and "zero-proof" have different (and, sometimes, legally regulated) definitions depending upon where you are in the world. Most people know that "proof" is a measure of alcohol in a beverage, on a scale from 0 to 200. "Zero-proof" means 0.0 percent alcohol by volume (ABV), a beverage completely free of alcohol.

"Nonalcoholic" and "alcohol-free" can be more nuanced terms. In the United States, beverages with up to 0.5 percent ABV can be labeled "nonalcoholic," but not "alcohol-free." "Alcohol-free" means 0.0 percent ABV in the United States so the terms "alcohol-free" and "zero-proof" can be used interchangeably. In the United Kingdom, however, beverages with up to 0.05 percent ABV can be labeled as "alcohol-free."

You might also see the term "dealcoholized" when looking for alcohol alternatives. This is common in nonalcoholic wines and beers. This means that alcohol is involved in the creation process of the beverage, but then removed at a later phase of the process. Since dealcoholized beverages often result in up to 0.5 percent ABV remaining in the final product, they can be labeled "nonalcoholic" in the United States. However, not all "nonalcoholic" beverages involve alcohol in the creation process. Some are crafted from scratch without any presence of alcohol, but may or may not develop small traces of alcohol during the creation process.

Why Terminology Matters

Why do these distinctions matter? Because even seasoned players in the market seem to misuse these terms in marketing contexts, especially "zero-proof." For example, because a "nonalcoholic" spirit in the United States could still have up to 0.5 percent ABV, you cannot call that drink either alcohol-free or zero-proof, as is sometimes done. Don't get me wrong: The term "zero-proof" is great, but you have to be careful when using it because zero means zero, not zero point five. It is important to know what these terms mean in your country because that small percentage of alcohol, even though minuscule, could have different meanings and importance to different people, especially those in recovery or with medical conditions.

INGREDIENTS TO HAVE ON HAND

The key to making great mocktails is using the best ingredients available. These include the quality of the alcohol-free and nonalcoholic spirits you select, as well as the fresh fruits, herbs, juices, and homemade syrups and sweeteners. The combination of these—and some creativity—will allow you to make complex and balanced mocktails that are sure to impress you and your guests.

Alcohol-Free and Nonalcoholic Spirits

Most of the available nonalcoholic spirits on the market today are crafted from the ground up using all-natural ingredients. A lot of them are allergen-free, and most are very low in calories; some are even zero-calorie.

But even with the many alternatives available, it is important to maintain realistic expectations concerning spirit alternatives. Alcohol and its physical qualities are difficult to replicate. For example, nonalcoholic spirits, in general, are not meant to be sipped neat like some liquors. They are instead meant to be combined with other flavors in a finished product such as a mocktail. For this reason, you'll find that many recipes in this book call for a proportion of nonalcoholic spirit that is *larger* than the proportion of an alcoholic spirit called for in a traditional cocktail recipe. This is to compensate for dilution and to let the natural flavors of the alternative spirit shine. The removal of the alcohol also affects a drink's texture, so one must find creative ingredients and methods to create texture in your mocktail. Finally, removing alcohol also risks sacrificing the burning sensation it provides when running down your throat. To compensate, some nonalcoholic spirits are spicy (using capsaicin), which can give your mocktail a kick without the booze, such as a tingling sensation up your nose that makes you want to go "Whoo!"

You may notice that this book does not feature a vodka alternative and that is because there are very few options out there. That is not surprising since vodka doesn't have a distinctive flavor—like juniper berries for gin, molasses for rum, or oak and vanilla for whiskey—it simply tastes like alcohol. In addition, like a good cocktail, a good mocktail will contain well-balanced flavors, and not simply replicate the flavor of alcohol. Achieving a well-balanced mocktail that mimics the taste of alcohol within the experience of a mixed drink can be done with the spirit alternatives and methods described in this book. Following are some popular nonalcoholic spirits.

Tequila

Tequila is a spirit made from the core of the blue agave plant called "piña." Some tequilas are fruity and citrusy while others are earthy and mineral-y. The majority of the tequila alternatives available have flavors of agave, capsicum, and lime, with a peppery finish. For a Reposado-style tequila alternative, Ritual Zero Proof Tequila Alternative is smoky and citrusy on the nose. It has nice black peppercorn and green bell pepper flavors that really give it a good kick. Free Spirits' The Spirit of Tequila is fruity and citrus forward on the palate with a mild sweetness. It also has a strong spicy finish. For a Blanco-style tequila alternative, Lyre's Agave Blanco Spirit is citrusy and a little floral on the nose. It has a zesty flavor and a mild peppery finish.

Gin

The most common type of gin, London dry gin, starts as a neutral grain spirit like vodka. Botanicals, including juniper berries, are then infused into the spirit for that distinct gin flavor. You'll find that most nonalcoholic gin spirits use juniper berries to give it that fragrant aroma and gin-like flavor. After all, gin without juniper berries is just vodka. Monday Zero Alcohol Gin is juniper forward both on the nose and in its flavor. Ritual Zero Proof Gin Alternative also has juniper flavors along with cucumber and peppers that give it a mild kick.

Rum

Rum is usually created from sugarcane or molasses. It goes through fermentation and distillation and is usually aged in oak barrels. Nonalcoholic rums pull inspiration from these classic rum components. For a light rum alternative, Lyre's White Cane Spirit provides a subtle, sweet flavor that is versatile. For a dark rum alternative, Ritual Zero Proof Rum Alternative is full-bodied and rich in flavor. It has hints of cinnamon, vanilla, and molasses.

Whiskey

Whiskey is made from fermented grain mash, usually barley, corn, rye, or wheat. It also goes through fermentation, distillation, and aging in wooden barrels. Once aged, it is blended with other whiskeys for a consistent flavor profile. Most nonalcoholic whiskey spirits have flavors of oak, vanilla, and caramel. Spiritless Kentucky 74 is distilled twice—first into a high-quality spirit, and then again to remove all of the alcohol. The resulting product tastes very close to real bourbon with a smooth finish and flavors of vanilla and caramel. Lyre's Traditional Reserve or Lyre's American Malt are also good options for a blended malt whisky with flavors of toffee and oak. They shine when mixed in mocktails, providing an aftertaste that is reminiscent of the real thing.

Aperitif

Aperitifs are usually served before a meal to stimulate the appetite and enhance the dining experience. The popular alcoholic aperitifs include Campari and Aperol. These two are similar but not the same. Campari has a beautiful crimson color and is richer, stronger, and a bit more bitter in flavor. Aperol has a bright orange color, and is a little less bitter and therefore sweeter. These two types of aperitifs have been an important part of mixology and are incorporated as key ingredients in a lot of cocktails. This book will refer to the Campari-type aperitif as Italian red aperitif and the Aperol-type aperitif as Italian orange aperitif.

Thankfully, there are now several nonalcoholic Italian aperitifs on the market. You need not miss out on Negronis and Aperol spritzes anymore just because you don't consume alcohol. For a nonalcoholic Italian red aperitif, Lyre's Italian Orange captures the essence of red Italian bitter aperitif with flavors of blood orange and orange pith. Free Spirits' The Spirit of Milano has flavors of bitter orange, is slightly sweet, and has a nice peppery finish. Ritual Zero Proof Aperitif Alternative is the most bitter and spicy of all the options tried. A little goes a long way. Its flavors will definitely hold up in mocktails, and are perfect for spritzes. Ghia's nonalcoholic aperitif has a nice balance of bitter and citrus flavors. It has a lingering heat without being spicy upfront. Like Ritual, a little Ghia goes a long way. For a nonalcoholic Italian orange aperitif, Lyre's Italian Spritz, like Aperol, is bright and bittersweet with a striking orange-red color.

Note that you can substitute Italian orange for Italian red—just be aware that Italian red is usually more bitter and richer in flavor so the quantities may need to be adjusted.

Wine

Using wine as a mocktail ingredient is a good way to add depth and complexity to your drink. Some wine cocktails use wine as the main ingredient and some use it as a component to enhance the overall flavor of the drink. The majority of the nonalcoholic wines on the market are dealcoholized. They use traditional winemaking methods and then remove alcohol later in the process. This helps to preserve flavors in the resulting nonalcoholic form.

Dealcoholized sparkling wines are becoming quite good and a lot of them taste like their alcoholic counterparts. The carbonation helps with the texture. Fre Sparkling Brut and Fre Sparkling Rosé are really good dealcoholized options to drink by themselves or to use in mocktails. Lyre's Classico is a nonalcoholic sparkling wine that's a great option for those who want to enjoy a bubbly wine that is built alcohol-free from scratch and not dealcoholized.

Red wine is more challenging to mimic so it is important to adjust expectations when it comes to this category. Removing the alcohol affects the texture of the drink and there is no carbonation to save it. Mixing nonalcoholic red wine with other ingredients in a mocktail will help with the overall flavor and texture. Thomson & Scott's Noughty Non-Alcoholic Rouge produced with Syrah grapes is great due to its dryness. It has tannins that contribute to the mouthfeel. Ariel's Dealcoholized Cabernet Sauvignon is also a good option. It is a bit fruitier, but it has that red wine aftertaste.

Bitters

Bitters are the "salt and pepper" of the mixology world. They improve cocktails by adding complexity while elevating the flavors of the other components in the drink. There's a wide range of bitters available on the market, from the classic Angostura bitters and Peychaud's bitters, to citrus bitters like orange bitters and grapefruit bitters. There are lavender bitters, tiki bitters, celery bitters—the list goes on.

The majority of the bitters available on the market have high alcohol content. However, since most cocktails that incorporate bitters use only a minuscule amount of it—usually, a couple of "dashes"—applying a couple of dashes of bitters to an otherwise nonalcoholic drink can still be classified as "nonalcoholic," depending on the volume used. One dash of bitters is usually between 0.8 and 0.9 milliliter. A dash is different from a drop, though. One dash of bitters is equivalent to six to eight drops. If you're using bitters with droppers, one full dropper is usually about 0.8 milliliter. Most droppers have milliliter measurements for ease of use.

If you're looking for fully alcohol-free bitters, a company called All The Bitter makes very complex bitters that taste much like their alcoholic counterparts. As of this writing, they have Aromatic, New Orleans, Orange, and Lavender bitters. The Aromatic Bitters have flavors of cinnamon, nutmeg, and clove perfect for classics like an old-fashioned or a Manhattan. The New Orleans Bitters, reminiscent of Peychaud's bitters, have flavors of cherry, anise, and hibiscus. The Orange Bitters is citrus forward with a little spice to it. The Lavender Bitters provide beautiful floral flavors from lavender, chamomile, and rose.

BASIC INGREDIENTS TO MAKE AHEAD

Following are some staple ingredients in many mocktails that can be made ahead of time and kept on hand.

Sweeteners

There are a number of ways to incorporate sweetness into mocktails through syrups. Syrups are essential when it comes to mixology because they enhance flavor to achieve a balanced taste.

- **Simple syrup** can easily be made using different sweeteners like white sugar for a clean taste, demerara sugar to get flavors of molasses, or sugar alternatives for low-calorie options. Simple syrups can also be infused with botanicals, herbs, fruits, and teas to name a few options.
- **Agave nectar** is great in margaritas and mocktails using nonalcoholic tequila.
- **Maple syrup** goes well with dark, smoky spirit alternatives like nonalcoholic whiskey.
- **Honey syrup** goes well with mocktails using nonalcoholic gin, like Bee's Knees.

Each of these options offers a unique taste experience that makes crafting mocktails exciting, and the possibilities are endless! Here are some sample recipes.

◈ Simple Syrup ◈

Simple Syrup is the most basic syrup that you need to learn how to make, and it is so...simple.

MAKES 1¹/₂ CUPS

1 cup sugar

1 cup water

1. Combine sugar and water in a small saucepan. Bring to a boil.
2. Reduce heat and simmer about 3 minutes until sugar is dissolved, stirring occasionally.
3. Turn off heat and let cool.
4. Transfer to a Mason jar or another airtight container. Store in refrigerator 2–3 weeks.

◈ Juniper Simple Syrup ◈

Perfect for mocktails with nonalcoholic gin, Juniper Simple Syrup is a good way to add sweetness while amplifying the botanical flavor of gin.

MAKES 1¹/₂ CUPS

1 cup sugar

1 cup water

2 tablespoons dried juniper berries

1. Combine sugar, water, and berries in a small saucepan. Bring to a boil.
2. Using a muddler or the back of a wooden spoon, lightly press on berries to release their flavors.
3. Reduce heat and simmer about 3 minutes until sugar is dissolved, stirring occasionally.
4. Turn off heat and let cool.
5. Using a fine-mesh strainer, strain the syrup into a Mason jar or another airtight container. Discard berries. Store in refrigerator 2–3 weeks.

Herb-Infused Simple Syrup

**This recipe offers three herb options (rosemary, basil, or mint).
Herb-infused simple syrups not only add sweetness to mocktails,
but they also add fresh botanical flavors.**

MAKES 1¹/₂ CUPS

1 cup sugar

1 cup water

¹/₄ cup fresh herbs (rosemary, basil, or mint)

1. Combine sugar, water, and herbs in a small saucepan. Bring to a boil.
2. Reduce heat and simmer about 3 minutes until sugar is dissolved, stirring occasionally.
3. Turn off heat and steep for 30 minutes.
4. Using a fine-mesh strainer, strain the syrup into a Mason jar or another airtight container. Discard herbs. Store in refrigerator 2–3 weeks.

Orange Simple Syrup

**Using Orange Simple Syrup is a good way to incorporate citrus flavors
without adding volume to mocktails already calling for simple syrup.**

MAKES 1¹/₂ CUPS

1 cup sugar

1 cup water

5 ounces orange peels (taken from 3 medium oranges)

1. Combine sugar, water, and orange peels in a small saucepan. Bring to a boil.
2. Reduce heat and simmer 3 minutes until sugar is dissolved, stirring occasionally.
3. Turn off heat and steep for 30 minutes.
4. Using a fine-mesh strainer, strain the syrup into a Mason jar or another airtight container. Discard peels. Store in refrigerator 2–3 weeks.

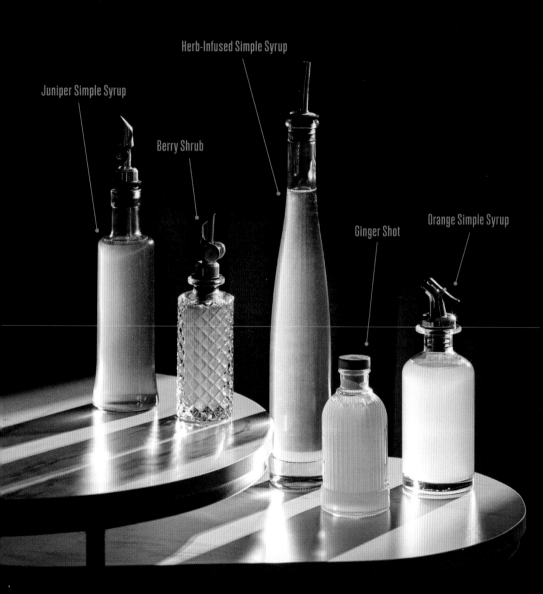

Juniper Simple Syrup

Herb-Infused Simple Syrup

Berry Shrub

Ginger Shot

Orange Simple Syrup

◈ Lavender Simple Syrup ◈

**A great way to add floral flavors to drinks is by using Lavender Simple Syrup.
This works great with citrus-forward and botanical mocktails.**

MAKES 1^1/$_2$ CUPS

1 cup sugar

1 cup water

3 tablespoons food-grade dried lavender

1. Combine sugar, water, and lavender in a small saucepan. Bring to a boil.

2. Reduce heat and simmer about 3 minutes until sugar is dissolved, stirring occasionally.

3. Turn off heat and steep for 10 minutes.

4. Using a fine-mesh strainer, strain the syrup into a Mason jar or another airtight container. Discard lavender. Store in refrigerator 2–3 weeks.

◈ Honey Syrup ◈

**Honey's thick consistency makes it hard to fully incorporate it into mocktails.
Adding a little bit of hot water into honey makes it easier to work with.**

MAKES ABOUT 1 CUP

^{1}/$_2$ cup honey

^{1}/$_4$ cup boiling water

1. Combine honey and water in a Mason jar.

2. Stir ingredients until well combined and honey is dissolved.

3. Store in refrigerator up to 2 weeks.

◈ Nonalcoholic Coffee Liqueur ◈

Some mocktails call for coffee liqueur. Thankfully, making a nonalcoholic version of it is simple and you can find all the ingredients at your grocery store or online!

MAKES 1 CUP

$\frac{1}{4}$ cup hot brewed coffee

1 teaspoon instant coffee

2 tablespoons dark brown sugar

$\frac{1}{2}$ cup hot water

2 tablespoons light corn syrup

3 tablespoons nonalcoholic imitation rum flavoring

1. In a large glass, combine brewed coffee, instant coffee, sugar, and water.

2. Mix until instant coffee and sugar are dissolved.

3. Add corn syrup and imitation rum flavoring and mix until well combined.

4. Let cool before using. Store in an airtight container and keep refrigerated up to 2 weeks.

◈ Low-Calorie Lemonade ◈

This lemonade recipe is lower in calories due to the use of monk fruit sweetener. Use this recipe instead of a store-bought lemonade if you want your mocktail to be guilt-free.

MAKES 5 CUPS

1 cup lemon juice

4 cups water

3 tablespoons monk fruit sweetener

1. In a medium pitcher, combine all ingredients and stir until monk fruit sweetener is dissolved.

2. Transfer to an airtight container and refrigerate. Use within 5–7 days.

◈ Ginger Shot ◈

Add a kick to your mocktails with ginger shots!
Ginger shots are very useful in mocktails. Use this recipe if ginger shots aren't available in your grocery store, or if you just want to save money by making your own. When using ginger shots in mocktails, you can skip the souring agent since most shots already include lemon juice.

MAKES 2 CUPS

1 pound unpeeled ginger root, washed, dried, and cut into small chunks
$2/3$ cup lemon juice
$1/4$ cup water
$1/4$ cup agave nectar

1. Place all ingredients into a blender or food processor.
2. Blend on high until smooth. Be sure to stop and scrape the sides of the blender or food processor.
3. Transfer the mixture to a large bowl lined with cheesecloth. Gather the corners of the cheesecloth. Twist and squeeze the juice out.
4. Continue squeezing until all of the liquid is expelled into the bowl.
5. Store in an airtight container. Refrigerate and use within 5–7 days.

◈ Berry Shrub ◈

Shrubs are flavored syrups that combine fruits, sugar, and vinegar.
But don't let the vinegar throw you off. The sour taste of vinegar is balanced out
by the fruit and sugar, and the vinegar's acidity mellows by the time the shrub is
ready to use. Making shrubs takes some preparation and time, usually about a
week, but it is worth the wait. A batch of shrub also has a long shelf life.
It can keep for weeks, even months, in the refrigerator. Shrubs can be
mixed with carbonated water and ice and enjoyed that way, or used
in a mocktail to add flavor and complexity.

MAKES 1^1/$_2$ CUPS

1 cup mixed fresh berries (blueberries and strawberries), washed and patted dry
1 cup granulated sugar
1 cup apple cider vinegar

1. In a medium airtight container, add berries and sugar.

2. Using a muddler or the back of a wooden spoon, muddle or crush berries. Mix crushed berries and sugar until well combined.

3. Cover container and refrigerate for 48 hours, mixing every 12 hours to make sure sugar is well combined with berries.

4. After 48 hours, the mixture should look very syrupy with most of the sugar dissolved.

5. Sterilize a Mason jar with lid.

6. Using a fine-mesh strainer or cheesecloth, strain berry and sugar mixture into the prepared Mason jar. Discard berries.

7. Mix in vinegar.

8. Cover the Mason jar and refrigerate at least 72 hours before tasting.

SUNDRY ADDITIONAL INGREDIENTS

The following are other ingredients that can be purchased and kept on hand.

Fresh Fruits

The easiest way to add freshness, sweetness, and even vitamins and minerals to your mocktail is by incorporating fresh fruits in it. There are lots of ways to get creative with fresh fruits in mocktails. You can mix and match berries, pair tropical fruits like pineapple or mango with nonalcoholic rum, or make different flavors of margarita by using muddled fruit in it.

Fresh Juices

Lemon and lime are the most common souring ingredients used in mocktails and cocktails. As much as possible, use fresh lemon or lime juice since that affects the overall taste of the drink. Using a hand juicer is the best way to get fresh juice at home. This method incorporates the oils from the citrus peel and the slight bitterness from the pith into the juice, adding layers of flavor into the drink. It is also best to use fresh fruit juices like orange, grapefruit, or pineapple when a mocktail recipe calls for it. If squeezing your own fresh juice is not possible, look for "fresh" juices in grocery stores. This is the next best thing, but note that some may have additives in them.

Dried Juniper Berries

Dried juniper berries are used in mocktails where there is nonalcoholic gin or where the flavor of gin is needed. This is because juniper berries give gin that woody, piney flavor and aroma. Using dried juniper berries helps amplify that aroma and flavor in mocktails to give the illusion that there's gin in the drink when there is none. Dried juniper berries can be purchased in the spice aisle of most grocery stores or you can buy them online. Although consuming dried juniper berries in moderation is generally considered safe for most people, it is best to consult with a healthcare professional before incorporating dried juniper berries into your mocktails.

Teas

Use concentrated tea to add herbal flavors, aroma, and color to mocktails. Some teas can also be astringent, which adds acidity to the drink. Some of the teas used in this book include hibiscus tea, butterfly pea flower tea, and ashwagandha tea—most of which are available in grocery stores or online.

Carbonated Drinks

Texture is important in mocktails. One way to incorporate texture into the drink is by adding some carbonation to it. Use club soda or sparkling water if you just want carbonation and volume with a neutral taste. Tonic water can be used to add a little bitterness. Ginger beer and ginger ale can be used to add a kick to the drink with the former being stronger than the latter. There are also light, diet, zero-calorie, or zero-sugar versions of tonic water, ginger beer, and ginger ale that can be used if desired.

BAR TOOLS AND TECHNIQUES

You will need some basic tools in your bar cart in order to craft mocktails with ease, along with proper techniques! This section contains some recommendations for both, which you can use to create delicious-tasting drinks.

Bar Tools

Bar tools are available from many retailers and vary in quality, but more expensive does not necessarily mean a better experience. Most mixologists figure out what works for them by trying out different manufacturers and brands. Following are the basic tools you will need.

Cocktail Shaker

Cocktail shakers are used to mix drinks that are shaken with ice. For home use, the cobbler shaker is the most popular type due to its "all-in-one" design. It consists of a metal tin or a glass, a built-in strainer, and a cap. In contrast, professional bartenders and mixologists often use Boston shakers. This two-piece type of shaker comes with a larger tin and a smaller tin (or a glass). It doesn't come with a strainer so a separate Hawthorne strainer is needed. Although it takes some practice to properly seal the two pieces together, and to easily open it, the Boston shaker is very easy to clean and use once you get the hang of it. If these shakers are not available to you, a simple Mason jar with a lid and a Hawthorne strainer will also do the trick.

Mixing Glass

Not all cocktails are shaken. This applies to mocktails too. If your mocktail is "spirit forward," like a nonalcoholic old-fashioned, you will want to use a mixing glass instead of a shaker. A mixing glass is a container that you can use to stir your drink with ice using a bar spoon. This chills the drink without overly diluting it. A Julep or Hawthorne strainer is typically used with a mixing glass to filter out the ice when pouring the drink.

Jigger

A jigger is a measuring device used in mixology. Think of it as your measuring cup, but for cocktails. Jiggers are traditionally dual-sided, usually holding 2 ounces on one side and 1 ounce on the other. There are also jiggers that are 1 ^{1}/2 ounces on one side and ^{3}/4 ounce on the other so it is important to pay attention to the jigger measurements when shopping for one.

Bar Spoon

A bar spoon is a long-handled spoon, usually with a spiral handle, to help you stir your drinks with ease. Some bar spoons have a flat end that can be used to muddle ingredients. Some have a teardrop end that can be used to crack ice. Most American bar spoons equal a standard teaspoon in volume so you can use it for measuring as well. It is truly a versatile tool and a must-have in your bar cart.

Muddler

Many cocktails and mocktails require muddled ingredients, usually fruits or herbs, to infuse some freshness into the drink. Muddlers are usually made of either wood or steel. Wooden muddlers are comfortable to use but can become stained and are difficult to sanitize. Steel muddlers are easy to clean and usually have "teeth" at the bottom for better muddling, but they can be slippery when wet. It really comes down to your personal preference. The back of a wooden spoon will also work great if you can't get your hands on a muddler.

Fine-Mesh Strainer

This is most often used as an additional filter when pouring drinks into the serving glass. When shaking martinis, for example, the built-in strainer of a cobbler shaker won't be able to catch all the small fragments of ice that a fine-mesh strainer can. If your drink contains muddled ingredients, a fine-mesh strainer ensures that all unwanted pieces are filtered out for a clean-looking mocktail. Supplementing the standard strainer of a cocktail shaker by pouring a drink mixture through a fine-mesh strainer is called double-straining.

Cocktail Picks

Using cocktail picks in garnishes is a fun way to make your mocktail look visually appealing. Use them to pierce cherries, citrus peels, or olives, and display them across the top of the glass. Cocktail picks come in fun designs as well.

Mixology Techniques

Now that you have the tools that you need, it is important to learn how best to use them. Before diving into these basic techniques, here are some tips to follow before you start shaking:

- Whether you're shaking or stirring a drink, it is always best to add all the ingredients into the shaker or mixing glass first before adding any ice. Adding ice first will dilute the ingredients as you are building the drink, so only add ice right before shaking or stirring.
- Don't use crushed ice for shaking. This dilutes the drink more than is needed. Use larger cubed ice instead.
- Carbonated ingredients should never be shaken because they will explode. You'd end up wearing the drink instead of drinking it. Add the carbonated ingredient last after the mixture is already poured into the serving glass.

Wet Shaking

A wet shake means you're shaking the ingredients *with ice*. When using a Boston shaker, add ice so that it is two-thirds or three-quarters of the way full. When using a cobbler shaker, adding ice so that it is halfway full works better since there is less space for ice to travel in a cobbler shaker. Both shakers should be shaken for 10–12 seconds, typically.

Dry Shaking

A dry shake simply means shaking the ingredients *without ice*. This allows ingredients like egg whites or aquafaba to fully combine with the other ingredients, resulting in a creamy, silky texture that gives the drink a nice foam. You would want to dry shake for a bit longer, usually 20–30 seconds. It is usually followed by a wet shake prior to pouring into your serving glass. For best results, only add $3/4$ ounce egg white to get the right amount of foam.

Regal Shaking

A regal shake is a technique credited to Theo Lieberman. A citrus peel is added into a shaker prior to shaking it with ice. The oils from the citrus peel blend into the drink while shaking, adding a hint of bitterness and citrus flavors without adding volume. This is a good technique to use if you don't have orange bitters available.

Rolling

Sometimes, shaking or stirring just doesn't do the trick. With thicker ingredients, rolling is a better way to combine them without diluting the drink. This is done using a Boston shaker. In the larger tin, combine all the ingredients of your mocktail. Put ice in the smaller tin and cover with a Julep strainer. Pour the contents of the larger tin over the smaller tin with the strainer. Then pour the mixture from the smaller tin back into the larger tin. Do this five times to chill the mocktail.

PRESENTATION

One of the most important aspects of making and enjoying mocktails is the presentation. Oftentimes, when you order a nonalcoholic version of a cocktail from a regular bar, the drink is served in a conspicuously big glass with little or no garnish. Nobody likes that, so we are going to change it! To elevate your mocktail experience, you'll need nice glassware and classy garnishes.

Glassware

Choosing the right glassware is important not only for the visual presentation but also for practical purposes. Some are used to keep drinks chilled without ice and some are meant to hold ice. This section contains basic information on commonly used glassware.

- **Martini glass (sometimes called cocktail glass):** A V-shaped stemmed glass used for cocktails that are strained and served without ice (served up). Usually holds 4–6 ounces.
- **Coupe glass:** Originally used for champagnes, coupe glasses are now more commonly used as a substitute for martini glasses for cocktails that are served up. It is a stemmed glass that has a classy, retro look. Usually holds 4–8 ounces.

- **Nick and Nora glass:** An elegant, vintage glassware that has a stem and is similar to a coupe glass but has a wider and more rounded bowl. It is also used for cocktails that are served up. Usually holds 6–8 ounces.
- **Rocks glass:** A rocks glass, sometimes called an old-fashioned glass or a tumbler, is a short glassware with a thick, wide base. It is used to serve cocktails over ice. A regular rocks glass usually holds 6–10 ounces while a double rocks glass usually holds 12–14 ounces.
- **Highball glass:** A highball glass is a tall narrow glassware typically used to serve cocktails with a large portion of nonalcoholic mixers like juice, soda, or tonic water. Usually holds 10–12 ounces.
- **Collins glass:** A Collins glass is similar to a highball glass, but it is taller and narrower. It is also used to serve drinks with a large portion of mixers. Usually holds 10–14 ounces.
- **Margarita glass:** A stemmed glassware with a wide, shallow bowl and a narrow stem. Usually holds 8–12 ounces, so it has plenty of room for ice.
- **Wine glass:** A stemmed glassware that can either have a wide bowl (red wine glasses) or a narrow bowl (white wine glasses). Usually holds 8–12 ounces.
- **Champagne flutes:** This glassware has a long, narrow bowl that tapers toward the top, and a stem that separates the bowl from the base. Usually holds 6–8 ounces.
- **Tiki glasses/mugs:** Typically used to serve tropical-themed mocktails, tiki glasses and mugs are often inspired by Polynesian art and culture and feature intricate designs. Usually holds 8–16 ounces.

Garnishes

After you mix up a great-tasting mocktail and present it in a fancy glass, garnishes are a great way to round up your other senses: sight and smell. Garnishes add to the overall experience by making your drink visually appealing and giving the drinker (through scent) a hint of the flavors they will taste in the mocktail. This section covers how to make some of the garnishes used in this book.

- **Citrus wedge, wheel, twist, or rose:** These are the easiest garnishes to incorporate into your drink, as most mocktails have a citrus ingredient. Peels can be presented in a variety of shapes that make drinks look more interesting. The citrus oils also add a subtle flavor to the drink while giving it a nice aroma.

- *Citrus wedge:* To make citrus wedges, slice the citrus fruit in half lengthwise (from one tip to the other tip). Slice each half again in the same manner, into quarters. Remove any seeds.
- *Citrus wheel:* To make citrus wheels, cut the citrus fruit horizontally into $1/4$"-thick slices. These cross-sections of the fruit give a "wheel" appearance.
- *Citrus twist:* Using a Y-shaped vegetable peeler, shave off a citrus peel that is about 1" wide and 3" long, and then twist it in opposite directions with your fingers. If you're going to put the peel into the drink, cut the edges so that the sides look straight.
- *Citrus rose:* To make a citrus "rose," peel a rind into a long continuous band and then roll it tightly onto itself like a snail shell to form a "rose." Pierce the rind through the center of the rose with a cocktail pick to hold its form.
- **Dehydrated citrus wheels:** These are good substitutes for fresh citrus wheels. They add an edgy look to the drink and are perfect for when you don't have fresh citrus on hand. Dehydrated citrus wheels can be purchased retail or made at home by baking fresh citrus wheels in the oven at a low temperature (200°F) for 4 hours. This is also a great way to save your citrus fruits that are about to go bad.
- **Fresh herbs:** When fresh herbs are used as garnish, they usually sit on top of the drink and therefore close to the nose of the drinker when the mocktail is sipped. This gives a nice fresh aroma and enhances the overall experience. Smack the fresh herbs lightly prior to adding them to your drink to activate their oils and scent. You can also use a small bouquet of herbs—a few pieces of herbs pinched or twisted together—as a garnish to give the drink a more refreshing, full look.
- **Fresh fruits and vegetables:** Fruits and vegetables are a nice way to add a fresh look to the drink, and can make a drink look even more appetizing.
    - *Apple fan:* Apple fans are a good way to garnish fall-themed drinks that have apple flavors. To make an apple fan, cut an apple into quarters. Take one quarter and cut a straight edge on the side that contained part of the core. Then slice the quarter from top to bottom into identical, thinner wedge shapes about $1/8$" thick. Stack these together, pierce one end with a cocktail pick, and then use the pick as a hinge to fan the wedges out.
    - *Strawberries:* A small strawberry can be used to garnish a drink. Just make a notch at the tip of the berry and fit the berry on the rim of your glass at the notch. The same can be done with strawberry slices as well.

- *Cucumber wheels and ribbons:* Make sure to wash your cucumbers thoroughly. Slice the cucumber crosswise to make $1/4$"-thick cucumber wheels. To make ribbons, using a Y-shaped vegetable peeler, peel the skin of a cucumber from one tip to the other. This will give you a long strip of cucumber skin. Discard that piece. Then peel the same area again from one tip to the other. This will yield a strip of cucumber for which the middle is from inside the cucumber, while the outer skin of the cucumber is still on the edge. Condense the ribbon into a "wave" and pierce it with a cocktail pick to hold the shape.
- *Cocktail cherries:* Cherries are classic garnishes that add sophistication to any drink. They can be presented on a cocktail pick or dropped directly into the drink. Cherries are often used in cocktails that are spirit forward to add a nice burst of sweetness. They are also commonly used in tropical drinks.
- *Pineapple frond:* Crowning a drink with a tall pineapple frond, or leaf, is a unique way to add excitement to a tropical drink. Pineapple fronds can also be frozen to prolong their shelf life.

PART 2

The Recipes

Now it's time to apply your knowledge from Part 1 and start mixing mocktails! In this part you will find seventy-five mocktail recipes, arranged into six chapters that each feature one of the main spirit alternatives, plus a seventh chapter featuring "spirit-free" recipes using common ingredients rather than dedicated spirit alternatives. From nonalcoholic takes on classic cocktails to unique and exciting flavor combinations, the hope is that you find mocktail recipes to enjoy without missing the alcohol.

CHAPTER 2

GIN-INSPIRED
MOCKTAILS

Gin alternatives are versatile, which makes them a perfect base for mocktails. The juniper and citrus notes mix beautifully with cocktails that include fresh herbs and fruits. You can also get creative by infusing your gin alternative with different types of tea. Infusing it with tea like butterfly pea flower not only gives it a nice color but also complements the botanical flavors of the spirit. You will also see that dried juniper berries are used in this chapter. These enhance the juniper flavors of your gin alternative and can give the impression that the drink contains real gin! Some gin alternatives also have a subtle peppery finish to mimic the burn that you get from alcohol. From flavorful martinis to refreshing fizzes, you'll find something to love whether you're wanting a moody cocktail during winter or you're looking to quench your thirst on a hot day.

Bee's Knees

The Bee's Knees is a Prohibition-era cocktail that uses honey to mask the smell of the homemade "bathtub gin" used when alcohol was illegal to purchase. In this version, some of the piney aromas associated with gin were intentionally retained. Incorporating juniper berries and a gin alternative helps capture the essence of the original drink without the alcohol.

SERVES 1

Ingredients

$1\frac{1}{2}$ ounces gin alternative

$\frac{3}{4}$ ounce lemon juice

$\frac{3}{4}$ ounce Honey Syrup
(see recipe in Chapter 1)

7 dried juniper berries

Mocktail Twist

Gin's distinctive scent is actually the scent of the juniper berry! Juniper berries are the one botanical required for gin to be called gin. Juniper berries are said to have antioxidant and anti-inflammatory properties. Their flavor is often described as piney and woodsy.

1. Place a Nick and Nora glass in the freezer, allowing it to chill as you prepare the mocktail. Using a chilled glass later on helps the drink to stay cold longer, especially since this drink is not served with ice. If you don't have a Nick and Nora glass, a coupe glass will also work well with this mocktail.

2. In a cocktail shaker, add gin alternative, lemon juice, Honey Syrup, and berries. If desired, you can lightly press on berries using a muddler to break them apart for a more juniper-forward taste.

3. Add large cubes of ice to the shaker, cover it, and shake vigorously 10–12 seconds or until the exterior of the shaker becomes frosty. The act of shaking also further breaks down the dried juniper berries, allowing their flavor to be released into the drink.

4. Using a fine-mesh strainer, double-strain the mixture into the chilled Nick and Nora glass. This step effectively filters out any remnants of berries, resulting in a smooth and refined mocktail. The Bee's Knees does not require any garnish, which makes the drink simple but elegant.

Lychee Elderflower Fizz

The lychee fruit is the star of this mocktail recipe. It provides a subtle sweetness and hints of floral flavors that work well with the botanicals of the gin alternative. The mint adds a burst of freshness that makes this drink perfect for hot summer days.

SERVES 1

Ingredients

4 lychee fruit (canned or fresh, peeled and seeded)

$1\frac{1}{2}$ ounces lychee syrup (if you're using canned lychees) or regular Simple Syrup (see recipe in Chapter 1)

$\frac{1}{2}$ ounce lime juice

2 ounces gin alternative

8 mint leaves

7.5 ounces elderflower tonic water

2–3 mint sprigs and 1 lychee fruit for garnish

Mocktail Twist

Lychee is a fruit native to Southeast Asia. This fruit has a delicious, mild flavor and is a good source of vitamin C and copper. Leftover canned lychee fruits will keep for several weeks if placed in an airtight container and refrigerated. Be sure to label their expiration date!

1. In a cocktail shaker, muddle 4 lychees and lychee syrup together. Add lime juice and gin alternative to the shaker.

2. Give mint leaves a nice slap on the palm of your hand, and then add them to the cocktail shaker. Note that you don't want to muddle the mint leaves with the fruit since that would release bitter flavors.

3. Add large cubes of ice to the shaker, cover it, and shake 10–12 seconds. The shaking releases the oils from the mint leaves without making the drink bitter.

4. Fill a double rocks glass $2/3$ full with ice cubes. Using a fine-mesh strainer, double-strain the mixture into the glass. This step filters out any remnants of lychee and mint leaves. Top with tonic water.

5. Make a mint bouquet by pinching or twisting mint sprigs together. Lightly slap the bouquet around the mouth of the glass to release its oils and aroma.

6. Garnish the drink with the mint bouquet and 1 lychee fruit, perhaps on a cocktail pick.

French Kiss

Drawing inspiration from the classic French 75 champagne cocktail, this mocktail is simple and easy to create even when you don't have nonalcoholic champagne available. The ginger ale really brings out the botanical flavors of the gin alternative and leaves a slight tingling sensation on your lips.

SERVES 1

Ingredients

2 ounces gin alternative

1/2 ounce grenadine

1/2 ounce lime juice

3 dashes alcohol-free Peychaud's-style bitters

3 ounces chilled ginger ale

1 maraschino cherry for garnish

Mocktail Twist

Peychaud's bitters are light and fruity with flavors of anise and cherry. They were created by Antoine Amédée Peychaud and originally produced in New Orleans, Louisiana. For an alcohol-free version of Peychaud's bitters, try All The Bitter's delicious New Orleans Bitters.

1. Place a martini glass in the freezer, allowing it to chill as you prepare the drink. This helps the drink retain its temperature later. This drink can also be served in a chilled coupe glass.

2. In a cocktail shaker, combine gin alternative, grenadine, lime juice, and bitters.

3. Add large cubes of ice to the shaker, cover it, and shake vigorously 10–12 seconds or until the exterior of the shaker becomes visibly frosty.

4. Using a fine-mesh strainer, double-strain the mixture into the chilled martini glass. This removes any small pieces of ice from the shaking as well as any lime seeds or pulp.

5. Carefully top with ginger ale, pouring slowly to prevent it from fizzing over.

6. Using a bar spoon, give the drink a light stir to combine the mixture with the ginger ale.

7. To garnish, use a paring knife to make a notch at the bottom of a cherry, then place cherry on the rim of the martini glass at the notch. You can also simply drop a cherry to the bottom of the drink.

Lavender Lemon Drop Martini

This delightful nonalcoholic cocktail not only tastes incredible but also presents a visual feast for the eyes! The gin alternative's herbal notes are elevated by the delicate floral essence of the Lavender Simple Syrup. The result is a balanced mocktail with hints of herb, sweetness, tartness, and floral undertones.

SERVES 1

Ingredients

2 ounces gin alternative

½ ounce lemon juice

¾ ounce Lavender Simple Syrup (see recipe in Chapter 1)

1 ounce butterfly pea flower tea (cooled to room temperature)

1 lemon peel and 1 lavender sprig for garnish

Mocktail Twist

If you'd like the martini a bit sweeter, you can sugar-rim half of the coupe glass. Do this by rubbing a lemon wedge against half of the coupe glass's rim to wet it, and then dipping that half of the rim into a small pile of sugar that has been spread onto a plate. Sugar rims make the drink appear more like the classic lemon drop martini.

1. Place a coupe glass in the freezer, allowing it to chill while you prepare the drink.

2. In a cocktail shaker, combine gin alternative, lemon juice, Lavender Simple Syrup, and tea.

3. Add large cubes of ice to the shaker, cover it, and shake vigorously approximately 8–10 seconds. This process cools the drink without diluting it too much.

4. To achieve a smooth texture, use a fine-mesh strainer to double-strain the mixture into the chilled coupe glass. This removes any small ice fragments and any lemon seeds or pulp.

5. Finally, garnish with lemon peel and lavender sprig for an extra touch of elegance.

Strawberry Gin Mule

Inspired by the classic Moscow mule, this mocktail uses a gin alternative instead of vodka, as well as strawberries for a fruity flavor. For a pleasant warming sensation while sipping this drink, use a ginger beer that is bold and spicy. For the ultimate mule experience, serve it in a copper mug.

SERVES 1

Ingredients

3 medium strawberries, chopped

1 ounce Simple Syrup (see recipe in Chapter 1)

1 ounce lime juice

2 ounces gin alternative

7 ounces ginger beer

2–3 mint sprigs, 1 dehydrated lime wheel, and $\frac{1}{2}$ strawberry for garnish

Mocktail Twist

Copper mugs are typically used to serve Moscow mules. It is a popular choice due to its attractive appearance and its ability to keep the drink frosty cold for a long time. They are also instantly recognizable and suggest that you know your mixology!

1. Combine chopped strawberries and Simple Syrup in a cocktail shaker and muddle them until the ingredients are well combined. Adding the syrup makes muddling the strawberries easier.

2. Add lime juice and gin alternative to the shaker.

3. Add large cubes of ice to the shaker, cover it, and shake vigorously 10–12 seconds or until the exterior of the shaker becomes visibly frosty.

4. Use a fine-mesh strainer and double-strain the mixture into a copper mug or a highball glass to remove any remnants of muddled strawberries and small pieces of ice. Alternatively, if you'd enjoy having small pieces of fruit in the drink, skip the straining step.

5. Top off the drink with ginger beer then fill the copper mug or highball glass with crushed ice using a scoop or a spoon.

6. Make a mint bouquet by twisting or pinching mint sprigs together and lightly slap it against the copper mug to release its oils and aroma. Garnish the drink with mint bouquet, lime wheel, and strawberry.

Citrus Rose Martini

This mocktail is inspired by a popular cocktail in the Philippines called the gin pomelo. Its popularity is partly due to the simplicity of its ingredients: pomelo-flavored powdered juice mix, water, gin, and ice. This martini version of the drink uses fresh grapefruit juice (since pomelos can be difficult to find).

SERVES 1

Ingredients

2 ounces gin alternative

1½ ounces fresh grapefruit juice

¾ ounce rose syrup

½ ounce lemon juice

1 grapefruit wedge or 1 edible flower for garnish

Mocktail Twist

Fresh grapefruit juice is always best for this drink, but if that is not in season or otherwise unavailable, you can buy grapefruit juice cans or jugs in most grocery stores. Rose syrups can be purchased online or in some liquor stores. If rose syrup is not available, you can substitute it with other floral syrups, for example lavender syrup will work beautifully with this mocktail as well.

1. Place a coupe glass in the freezer, so it becomes chilled while you prepare the drink.

2. In a cocktail shaker, combine gin alternative, grapefruit juice, rose syrup, and lemon juice.

3. Add large cubes of ice to the shaker, cover it, and shake 10–12 seconds or until the exterior of the shaker becomes visibly frosty.

4. Using a fine-mesh strainer, double-strain the mixture into the chilled coupe glass. This filters out any pulp or seeds and small pieces of ice.

5. For the finishing touch, garnish the mocktail with either grapefruit wedge or edible flower.

Cala-Martini

Calamansi, or Philippine lime, is a small but mighty citrus fruit. It is very sour and slightly bitter, making it perfect for mocktails. The Cala-Martini mocktail highlights this flavor, with Orange Simple Syrup to balance the tartness, along with orange bitters. These ingredients work in perfect concert with the gin alternative's herbal notes.

SERVES 1

Ingredients

2 ounces gin alternative

1 ounce Orange Simple Syrup (see recipe in Chapter 1)

¾ ounce calamansi juice

3 dashes alcohol-free orange bitters

1 calamansi wheel or 1 lime peel for garnish

Mocktail Twist

You can buy fresh calamansi fruit or frozen calamansi juice from most Asian grocery stores. If it is not available, you can substitute it with 1 ounce lime juice and add another dash of alcohol-free orange bitters. Regular orange bitters can also be used if you're comfortable with a little bit of alcohol.

1. Place a coupe glass in the freezer, ensuring it becomes chilled while you prepare the drink. You can also use a martini glass or a Nick and Nora glass.

2. In a cocktail shaker, combine gin alternative, Orange Simple Syrup, juice, and bitters.

3. Add large cubes of ice to the shaker, cover it, and shake 10–12 seconds or until the outside of the shaker becomes visibly frosty.

4. Using a fine-mesh strainer, double-strain the mixture into the chilled coupe glass. This step effectively filters out any small ice fragments, resulting in a smooth and refined mocktail.

5. Finally, garnish with calamansi wheel or lime peel on the rim of the glass.

Cucumber G&T

One way to incorporate flavors into your mocktail without
adding volume is by infusing your nonalcoholic spirits with something flavorful.
This mocktail uses nonalcoholic gin infused with cucumber slices to get subtle
yet refreshing flavors into the drink. It is important to choose a high-quality tonic
water for this recipe since that is the dominant ingredient.

SERVES 1

Ingredients

2 (¼"-thick) cucumber wheels

2 ounces gin alternative

½ ounce lime juice

7½ ounces tonic water

2–3 mint sprigs and 1 cucumber
   wheel for garnish

Mocktail Twist

You can also make a bigger batch
of the cucumber-infused gin
alternative and store it for later,
up to 3 days. The ratio is one ¼"
slice of cucumber for every ounce
of gin alternative.

1. Combine 2 cucumber wheels and gin alternative in a small jar. Cover it and set aside at least 1 hour. After the hour, extract and discard cucumber.

2. Unlike many mocktails, this drink is built in the very same glass in which you will serve it. To build the drink, add cucumber-infused gin alternative, lime juice, and tonic water to a highball glass.

3. Add a few cubes of ice and lightly stir to combine the ingredients.

4. Make a mint bouquet by twisting or pinching mint sprigs together and slap it against the rim of the highball glass to release its oils and aroma. Garnish drink with mint bouquet and 1 cucumber wheel.

Flower Sour

This drink not only looks beautiful but also has remarkable flavors and texture. The floral notes from the Lavender Simple Syrup work in perfect harmony with the herbaceous flavors of the butterfly pea flower tea–infused gin alternative.

SERVES 1

Ingredients

2 ounces butterfly pea flower tea–infused gin alternative (see sidebar)

1 ounce Lavender Simple Syrup (see recipe in Chapter 1)

1½ ounces butterfly pea flower tea (cooled to room temperature)

¾ ounce lemon juice

2 dashes alcohol-free Peychaud's-style bitters

¾ ounce egg white

1 lavender sprig for garnish

Mocktail Twist

Infuse your gin alternative with butterfly pea flower tea by putting a butterfly pea flower tea bag in 6 ounces of gin alternative and steeping it for 2 hours. You'll need 2 ounces for this drink, and you can save the remaining infused gin for making another Flower Sour or in another drink like the Lavender Lemon Drop Martini.

1. Place a Nick and Nora glass in the freezer, allowing it to chill. A coupe glass or martini glass will also work.

2. In a cocktail shaker, combine tea-infused gin alternative, Lavender Simple Syrup, tea, lemon juice, and bitters.

3. Using a jigger, measure ¾ ounce egg white and add that to the shaker. (Measuring the egg white precisely is important because a larger egg may have too much egg white. Failing to measure can produce an imbalanced drink with too much foam.)

4. Without adding any ice, cover the shaker and dry shake vigorously for 20 seconds.

5. Add large cubes of ice to the shaker, cover it, and wet shake another 10 seconds.

6. Using a fine-mesh strainer, double-strain the mixture into the chilled Nick and Nora glass.

7. Finally, garnish the mocktail with lavender sprig.

Blackberry Gin Basil Smash

A smash is a cocktail composed of a base spirit, citrus juice, sweetener, and herbs. This mocktail has all of these elements, using basil as the herb and blackberries to add flavor, color, and texture to the drink.

SERVES 1

Ingredients

6 medium blackberries

1 ounce Simple Syrup (see recipe in Chapter 1)

¾ ounce lemon juice

2 ounces gin alternative

6 basil leaves

1 ounce club soda

1 blackberry and 2 basil leaves for garnish

Mocktail Twist

If you'd like the blackberries and basil leaves directly in the drink, do a "dirty dump" by directly pouring all the contents of your shaker—including the spent ice and muddled fruit—into the glass. Consider also using a wider straw that will accommodate the pieces of fruit and herbs.

1. Combine 6 blackberries and Simple Syrup in a cocktail shaker. (Putting the syrup in with the berries makes muddling easier.)

2. Using a muddler or the back of a wooden spoon, press into blackberries, crushing the fruit into small pieces.

3. Add lemon juice and gin alternative to the shaker.

4. Grab 6 basil leaves, give them a nice slap to release their oils, then tear them into halves and add to the shaker.

5. Add large cubes of ice to the shaker, cover it, and shake 10–12 seconds. This step not only chills the drink but also releases the oils from the herbs, incorporating them into the mixture.

6. Fill a double rocks glass ⅔ full with ice cubes.

7. Using a fine-mesh strainer, double-strain the mixture into the glass. This filters out any remnants of fruit and herbs.

8. Carefully top the mixture with club soda, pouring slowly to prevent it from fizzing over.

9. Give the drink a light stir so that the mixture and club soda are well combined.

10. Garnish with 1 blackberry and 2 basil leaves on a cocktail pick.

Grapefruit Lavender Cooler

The tang and bitterness of freshly squeezed grapefruit juice harmoniously complements the subtle floral essence of the Lavender Simple Syrup, creating a truly refreshing and relaxing drink! As an option, you can add 1 ounce or more of club soda or carbonated water to the final drink before adding ice for a refreshing bit of carbonation and texture in the drink.

SERVES 1

Ingredients

2 ounces gin alternative

2 ounces fresh grapefruit juice

½ ounce lemon juice

½ ounce Lavender Simple Syrup (see recipe in Chapter 1)

3 dashes alcohol-free lavender bitters

1 grapefruit slice and 1 lavender sprig for garnish

Mocktail Twist

Lavender bitters can be bought online or at many liquor stores. There are alcohol-free options for lavender bitters as well. If these are unavailable, orange bitters can be used as a substitute in this drink.

1. Combine gin alternative, grapefruit juice, lemon juice, Lavender Simple Syrup, and bitters in a cocktail shaker.

2. Add large cubes of ice, cover the shaker, and shake vigorously 10–12 seconds. This step aerates the drink while also chilling and slightly diluting it.

3. Fill a double rocks glass ⅔ full with ice cubes.

4. Using a fine-mesh strainer, double-strain the mixture into the glass. This effectively filters out any small fragments of ice, as well as any juice pulps and seeds.

5. Garnish with grapefruit slice and lavender sprig laid on top of the glass.

CHAPTER 3

RUM-INSPIRED MOCKTAILS

There are many kinds of rum and, fortunately, there are also a variety of nonalcoholic rum options. Non-alcoholic light rum is versatile and can take the place of vodka in many mocktails. Dark rum alternatives have rich flavors of vanilla, toffee, and molasses. Dark rum's notes of vanilla, molasses, and cinnamon work perfectly with tropical fruit flavors like pineapple and mango. It is also a great way to add a kick to frozen mocktails like frozen daiquiris and piña coladas. It also works very well in complex and strong drinks like daiquiris and rum-tinis. Nonalcoholic spiced rum, like dark rum, has warm spices that include cinnamon, clove, and vanilla. From drinks inspired by the relaxed vibes of a far-away island to drinks that you'd find in a dark and moody speakeasy, there's a rum mocktail for every occasion.

Tiki Friday

**This tiki-style drink is sweet, fresh, and finishes with a kick!
The Tiki Friday draws inspiration from the Royal Hawaiian Mai Tai, a version
of the Mai Tai that features fresh orange and pineapple juices.**

SERVES 1

Ingredients

2 ounces rum alternative

1 ounce lime juice

1 ounce fresh orange juice

$1\frac{1}{2}$ ounces pineapple juice

$\frac{1}{2}$ ounce orgeat syrup

2–3 mint sprigs and 1 spent lime shell (hollowed-out half of a lime rind) for garnish

Mocktail Twist

The mai tai became so popular back in the 1940s and 1950s that it is believed to have depleted the worldwide rum supply! Fresh pineapple juice is preferred for this drink but unless you have a juicer, this can be challenging, so canned pineapple juice will also work. Just make sure that you choose a pineapple juice that is not from concentrate.

1. In a cocktail shaker, combine rum alternative, lime juice, orange juice, pineapple juice, and orgeat syrup.

2. Add large cubes of ice to the shaker, cover it, and shake 12–15 seconds. This is longer than usual, but allows for greater dilution, which this drink needs.

3. Strain the mixture into a tiki glass, then fill it with crushed ice using a scoop or spoon.

4. Create a mint bouquet by pinching or twisting mint sprigs together. Slap it against the tiki glass to release its oils and aroma.

5. Garnish the mocktail with mint bouquet, then add lime shell next to it. The lime shell represents an island and the mint bouquet represents palm trees on the island. This is how mai tais are traditionally garnished.

Regal Daiquiri

A daiquiri is a cocktail made with rum, citrus juice, and sweetener.
This recipe uses a dark rum alternative and demerara syrup. The flavor of
molasses from the demerara syrup plays really well with the vanilla and
toasted spice notes of the rum. You can also use this recipe as a basic
template to create your own daiquiri recipes!

SERVES 1

Ingredients

1 ounce lime juice

¾ ounce demerara syrup
(see Simple Syrup recipe in
Chapter 1)

2 ounces dark rum alternative

1 orange peel

1 lime wheel for garnish

Mocktail Twist

The structure ratio of a daiquiri
is usually 2:1:1 with the spirit
being twice the volume of the
sweetening and souring agents,
respectively. This ratio can
be adjusted depending on the
sweetener used, and is a great
template to use when inventing
your very own mocktail recipes.

1. Place a Nick and Nora glass in the freezer, ensuring
it becomes chilled while you prepare the drink.

2. In a cocktail shaker, combine lime juice, demerara
syrup, rum alternative, and orange peel.

3. Add large cubes of ice to the shaker, cover it, and
shake vigorously 10–12 seconds or until the mixture
is thoroughly chilled.

4. Using a fine-mesh strainer, double-strain the
mixture into the chilled Nick and Nora glass. This
step effectively filters out any small ice fragments,
resulting in a smooth and refined mocktail.

5. Finally, garnish the glass with lime wheel.

Tropical Heat

Coconut and ginger together? Yes! The gentle sweetness of coconut complements the earthy and fiery notes of ginger, creating a nice flavor combination. To round out the flavors, the rum alternative is added to introduce hints of vanilla and molasses, adding a layer of complexity in every sip!

SERVES 1

Ingredients

2 ounces coconut water

2 ounces dark rum alternative

1 ounce ginger syrup

½ ounce lime juice

1 slice fresh, unpeeled ginger for garnish

Mocktail Twist

You can make your own ginger syrup by following the steps for the Orange Simple Syrup recipe in Chapter 1, swapping out the orange peel for 8 ounces sliced fresh, unpeeled ginger. You can also buy ginger syrups online.

1. Place a coupe glass in the freezer, ensuring it becomes chilled while you prepare the drink.

2. In a cocktail shaker, combine coconut water, rum alternative, ginger syrup, and lime juice.

3. Add in large cubes of ice, cover the shaker, and shake 10–12 seconds. This step aerates and chills the mixture at the same time.

4. To filter out any small fragments of ice, use a fine-mesh strainer to double-strain the mixture into the chilled coupe glass.

5. Finally, garnish this mocktail with ginger on a cocktail pick.

Piña Colada

Virgin piña coladas, although tasty, are usually on the sweeter side. Good mocktails need something to balance the sweetness and add complexity. This version uses frozen pineapple chunks for added texture, and also uses a dark rum alternative that gives it a nice kick! You can use fresh pineapple chunks in place of the frozen pineapple chunks.

SERVES 1

Ingredients

½ cup frozen pineapple chunks

2 ounces pineapple juice

1 ounce cream of coconut

1 ounce coconut milk

2 ounces dark rum alternative

1 cup crushed ice

3 pineapple fronds and
   3 maraschino cherries
   for garnish

Mocktail Twist

Storing pineapple fronds is easy and provides a handy option for creating garnishes. After removing the fronds from the pineapple, clean and store them in a resealable plastic bag in the freezer. When you need them, just put the fronds under cool running water and they will look fresh again.

1. Put a highball glass in the freezer, allowing it to chill as you prepare the drink. Extra points if you have a pineapple-shaped glass!

2. Place pineapple, pineapple juice, cream of coconut, coconut milk, rum alternative, and ice in a blender. Blend until smooth. If it is too thick, add more pineapple juice.

3. Using a spatula or a bar spoon, scoop the mixture into the chilled highball glass.

4. To garnish, stick pineapple fronds on top of the drink and finish with cherries on a cocktail pick.

5. Add a fancy straw and enjoy this fantastic mocktail that is both refreshing and delicious!

Mango Rum Cooler

If you like tropical flavors, this might be the perfect mocktail for you.
Rum is closely associated with tropical islands, and most rum alternatives
replicate the distinctive taste of rum by incorporating rich flavors of molasses.
The fruity goodness of mango—also associated with tropical islands—
happens to complement these flavors beautifully.

SERVES 1

Ingredients

3 ounces mango juice

1$\frac{1}{2}$ ounces dark rum alternative

$\frac{1}{4}$ ounce lime juice

$\frac{1}{2}$ ounce Simple Syrup
(see recipe in Chapter 1)

2 ounces club soda

3–4 mango slices for garnish

Mocktail Twist

As a shortcut, skip the shaker and build this drink in the same glass you'll use to serve it. Add all ingredients except club soda into the glass, stir until well combined, add a few ice cubes, then top with club soda and garnish.

1. Place a double rocks glass in the freezer, allowing it to chill as you prepare the mocktail. This helps the drink to stay cold longer.

2. Combine mango juice, rum alternative, lime juice, and Simple Syrup in a cocktail shaker.

3. Add large cubes of ice, cover the shaker, and shake vigorously 10–12 seconds. This makes sure that all ingredients are well combined, aerated, and chilled.

4. Fill the chilled double rocks glass $\frac{2}{3}$ full with ice cubes.

5. Strain the mixture into the glass.

6. Top the mixture with club soda, then give it a light stir to combine.

7. Garnish with mango slices. (To give it an extra flair, turn your mango slices into a mango fan. You can use the same technique used to make an apple fan garnish described in Chapter 1 with mangoes as well!)

Espresso Rum-Tini

The story of the classic espresso martini is an interesting one.
Legend has it that a fashion model asked bartender Dick Bradsell for something
to "wake her up and f*** her up!" The espresso martini was the result. You can use
either a nonalcoholic light rum for a clean-tasting Espresso Rum-Tini or a dark/
spiced rum alternative to get flavors of warm spices that work well with coffee.
You can also buy nonalcoholic coffee liqueur online or in some liquor stores.

SERVES 1

Ingredients

2 ounces rum alternative

$1\frac{1}{2}$ ounces Nonalcoholic Coffee Liqueur (see recipe in Chapter 1)

$1\frac{1}{2}$ ounces chilled espresso (or cold brew concentrate)

$\frac{1}{2}$ ounce Simple Syrup (see recipe in Chapter 1)

3 coffee beans for garnish

Mocktail Twist

The classic three-coffee-bean garnish in an espresso martini is said to represent health, wealth, and happiness.

1. Place a martini glass or a coupe glass in the freezer, allowing it to chill as you prepare the mocktail. This is an important step because it will help keep the drink cold longer.

2. In a cocktail shaker, combine rum alternative, coffee liqueur, espresso, and Simple Syrup.

3. Add large cubes of ice to the shaker, cover it, and shake vigorously 12–15 seconds. Shaking it vigorously releases the oils from the espresso and produces a nice foam on top of the mocktail.

4. Using a fine-mesh strainer, double-strain the mixture into the chilled martini glass or coupe glass. This step effectively removes any small ice fragments, leaving a smooth and velvety Espresso Rum-Tini.

5. Finally, garnish by floating coffee beans on the foam.

Golden Fruit Daiquiri

Mango and cinnamon is a flavor pairing that should be as well known as peanut butter and jelly, and if you serve enough of these mocktails, perhaps it will be! The fruity goodness of the mango blends with the molasses flavor from the rum alternative, and is then complemented by a touch of cinnamon.

SERVES 1

Ingredients

1½ ounces rum alternative

2 ounces mango juice

½ ounce lime juice

¼ ounce Simple Syrup
(see recipe in Chapter 1)

1 tablespoon granulated sugar
for glass rim

1 teaspoon ground cinnamon for
glass rim

1 lime wedge for glass rim

1 mango slice for garnish

Mocktail Twist

When shopping for mango juice, look for those that are not from concentrate. For maximum freshness, you can also make your own mango juice by using a juicer, or by blending a mango with coconut water and then straining with a fine-mesh strainer.

1. Place a Nick and Nora glass in the freezer, allowing it to chill as you prepare the mocktail. A coupe glass or martini glass will work too.

2. Combine rum alternative, mango juice, lime juice, and Simple Syrup in a cocktail shaker.

3. Add large cubes of ice to the shaker, cover it, and shake 10–12 seconds or until the exterior of the shaker becomes frosty.

4. Combine sugar and cinnamon on a small plate.

5. Take the chilled Nick and Nora glass and wet half the rim of the glass using lime wedge. Dip wet rim in cinnamon-sugar mixture.

6. Using a fine-mesh strainer, double-strain the mixture into the chilled and rimmed Nick and Nora glass. This step effectively filters out any small fragments of ice, resulting in a smooth and refined mocktail.

7. Garnish with mango slice placed on the rim of the glass.

Ginger Bee

This mocktail can only be described as "soothing." Its combination of honey and citrus produces a delicious-tasting drink. The subtle tingling sensation from the ginger ale also adds a layer of fizzy texture to round out the drink.

SERVES 1

Ingredients

2 ounces light rum alternative

½ ounce lime juice

½ ounce Honey Syrup (see recipe in Chapter 1)

4 ounces ginger ale

1 lime "rose" for garnish (see instructions in Chapter 1)

Mocktail Twist

If you want a stronger drink, you can substitute the ginger ale with ginger beer. If ginger is not your thing, you can also use lemon-lime soda. To make this a low-calorie drink, use a zero-sugar or zero-calorie ginger ale. It will give you the same flavor profile without all the calories.

1. In a cocktail shaker, add rum alternative, lime juice, and Honey Syrup.

2. Add large cubes of ice, cover the shaker, and shake vigorously 12–15 seconds or until the exterior of the shaker becomes visibly frosty. This step makes sure that the Honey Syrup is well incorporated with the rest of the ingredients, which can be tricky.

3. Fill a Collins glass or a highball glass ⅔ full with ice cubes.

4. Strain the mixture into the glass.

5. Top with ginger ale then give it a light stir to combine.

6. Garnish with lime rose, add a nice straw, and enjoy.

Autumn Sparkler

The Autumn Sparkler draws inspiration from a mimosa but uses ginger ale instead of champagne. For an extra flair, serve it in a champagne flute rimmed with cinnamon sugar. This highlights the hints of toasted cinnamon and cloves coming from the dark rum alternative.

SERVES 1

Ingredients

1 tablespoon granulated sugar for glass rim

1 teaspoon ground cinnamon for glass rim

1 teaspoon Simple Syrup (see recipe in Chapter 1) for glass rim

1 ounce dark rum alternative

2 ounces chilled apple cider

4 ounces ginger ale

Mocktail Twist

For an even stronger ginger flavor, you can use a ginger beer that's bold and spicy in place of the ginger ale. You can also make this drink a nonalcoholic apple cider mimosa! Use a nonalcoholic sparkling brut in place of the ginger ale.

1. On a small plate, combine sugar and cinnamon. Pour the Simple Syrup onto a separate small plate.

2. Wet half the rim of a champagne flute by dipping it in Simple Syrup.

3. Dip the wet rim into cinnamon-sugar combination. Set the champagne flute aside.

4. Using a Boston shaker, combine rum alternative, apple cider, and ginger ale in the larger tin.

5. Put large cubes of ice in the smaller tin of the shaker, then place the Hawthorne strainer over it.

6. Using the rolling technique (see Chapter 1), pour the contents of the larger tin over the smaller tin with the strainer. Then gently pour the mixture from the smaller tin back into the larger tin, holding the ice back with the strainer. Do this four more times to effectively combine and chill the mixture.

7. Pour the mixture into the cinnamon sugar–rimmed champagne flute.

Holiday Punch

Most dark rum alternatives have notes of vanilla and warm spices. Combine this with flavors of cranberry and ginger and it will definitely remind you of the holiday season. Aside from flavors that are reminiscent of cheerful holiday moods, there is also a tingling and warming sensation from the ginger beer. Although an iced drink, it still offers a soothing and relaxing vibe.

SERVES 1

Ingredients

2 ounces dark rum alternative

1/2 ounce Simple Syrup
(see recipe in Chapter 1)

1/2 ounce lime juice

1 ounce cranberry juice

3 ounces ginger beer

1 lime wheel and 1 cocktail
cherry for garnish

Mocktail Twist

You can substitute the ginger beer with ginger ale for a more subtle flavor. Tonic water can also be used as a substitute for a slightly bitter flavor.

1. In a cocktail shaker, combine rum alternative, Simple Syrup, lime juice, and cranberry juice.

2. Add large cubes of ice, cover the shaker, and shake vigorously 10–12 seconds. Shaking not only chills and dilutes the drink but it also tames the acidity of the lime juice a little bit.

3. Fill a double rocks glass 2/3 full with ice cubes.

4. Strain the mixture into the glass.

5. Top with ginger beer.

6. Garnish with lime wheel and cocktail cherry. For an extra flair, create a citrus flag garnish. A citrus flag is a citrus wheel wrapped around a cherry, pierced with a cocktail pick.

Tropical Ginger Smash

There is a noticeable heat in this drink provided by the ginger shot!
Ginger shots are available in many grocery stores or you can make your
own using the recipe in Chapter 1. If you can't find cherry syrup, you can
use the syrup from a jar of bright red maraschino cherries.

SERVES 1

Ingredients

2 ounces dark rum alternative

$1/2$ ounce Ginger Shot (see recipe
in Chapter 1)

2 ounces pineapple juice

$1/2$ ounce cherry syrup

1 pineapple frond and
1 maraschino cherry
for garnish

Mocktail Twist

Make this drink even more
exciting by serving it in a clear
tiki glass. You can buy tiki
glasses and mugs online, but if
you're lucky, you can also find
them in thrift stores with a much
lower price tag.

1. Combine rum alternative, Ginger Shot, pineapple juice, and cherry syrup in a cocktail shaker.

2. Add large cubes of ice to the shaker, cover it, and shake vigorously 10–12 seconds.

3. Fill a double rocks glass $2/3$ full with small cubes of ice.

4. Strain the mixture into the glass.

5. Garnish with pineapple frond and cherry.

CHAPTER 4

TEQUILA-INSPIRED MOCKTAILS

If it's your first time dabbling in the world of spirit alternatives, pick a tequila alternative first. There are many different kinds of tequila alternatives, but the best ones are earthy, smoky, and spicy. Why? Because they hold up their flavors when mixed in mocktails. Some of the recipes in this chapter have a real "burn" that will make you question whether these are indeed nonalcoholic.

This chapter gives you plenty of margarita recipes—classic, frozen, served up. Sweeteners like agave nectar are sometimes used to extend that agave flavor that you get from tequila. Orange Simple Syrup is also used in some recipes that traditionally have triple sec and simple syrup, which are common ingredients in alcoholic margaritas. Aside from margaritas, you will also find reimagined classics like new takes on the Mexican Firing Squad, El Diablo, Paloma, and even an espresso martini.

Frozen Strawberry Margarita

This mocktail is fresh, delicious, fruity, and tastes like a real margarita thanks to the tequila alternative. Using a tequila alternative is key because it gives you that elevating "bump" that makes this taste like an adult drink. It is also what makes this different from a fruit shake.

SERVES 1

Ingredients

5 medium strawberries, chopped into quarters

1 ounce lime juice

1½ ounces fresh orange juice

1 ounce Simple Syrup (see recipe in Chapter 1)

2 ounces tequila alternative

1 cup crushed ice

1 tablespoon sea salt for glass rim

1 lime wedge for glass rim

1 lime wheel and 1 small strawberry for garnish

Mocktail Twist

Did you know that the frozen margarita's origin can be traced back to Dallas, Texas? It was invented by Mariano Martinez, who got the idea from a 7-Eleven Slurpee machine!

1. Place a margarita glass in the freezer, allowing it to chill as you prepare the mocktail. This will help the frozen margarita stay cold for longer.

2. In a blender, add chopped strawberries, lime juice, orange juice, Simple Syrup, and tequila alternative. Add crushed ice, cover the blender, and blend until smooth.

3. Place salt on a small plate. Grab the chilled margarita glass from the freezer and wet half the rim using lime wedge. Dip that wet part of the rim in salt. (Only partially rimming the glass with salt gives you and your guests the option to enjoy your margarita with or without salt.)

4. Pour the mixture into the salt-rimmed chilled margarita glass.

5. Finally, garnish with lime wheel and strawberry placed on an unsalted part of the rim of the margarita glass.

Fiery Squad

Inspired by the cocktail called Mexican Firing Squad, this mocktail truly packs a punch and is perfect for those who are looking for a strong nonalcoholic drink. The "burn" comes from the ginger syrup and tequila alternative, which has agave flavors with a spicy finish. The alcohol-free aromatic bitters bind all the flavors together, resulting in a mocktail so strong you may think there's alcohol in it.

SERVES 1

Ingredients

2 ounces tequila alternative

3 dashes alcohol-free aromatic bitters

1/2 ounce ginger syrup

1/4 ounce grenadine

3/4 ounce lime juice

1 lime wedge and 1 cocktail cherry for garnish

Mocktail Twist

The recipe for the Mexican Firing Squad cocktail was first published in *The Gentleman's Companion* written by the historian Charles H. Baker. He discovered this cocktail at La Cucaracha, a bar in Mexico City. The recipe is relatively simple to make, but the drink itself has layers of complexity.

1. Combine tequila alternative, bitters, ginger syrup, grenadine, and lime juice in a cocktail shaker.

2. Add large cubes of ice, cover the shaker, and shake vigorously 10–12 seconds or until the exterior of the shaker becomes visibly frosty.

3. Fill a double rocks glass 2/3 full with ice cubes.

4. Strain the mixture into the glass.

5. Garnish with lime wedge and cherry.

Unholy

This mocktail draws inspiration from the cocktail invented by
Trader Vic called El Diablo. The original recipe calls for crème de cassis,
which is a black currant liqueur. This recipe uses a small amount of black currant
concentrate in place of the crème de cassis, which adds a touch of sweetness
and color to make it look and taste like an El Diablo.

SERVES 1

Ingredients

2 ounces tequila alternative

1/2 ounce lime juice

1/2 ounce black currant concentrate

3 ounces ginger beer

1 dehydrated lime wheel for garnish

Mocktail Twist

Liqueurs are often sweet and flavored. They are made by infusing spirits with fruits, herbs, flowers, or other flavorings. If you're trying to replicate a cocktail that has a liqueur, find out what the flavor of that liqueur is and infuse your mocktail with that flavor. You can use infused simple syrups, muddled fruits, juices, or concentrates. Just make sure to adjust the volume of your substitute to ensure that your drink is not overly sweet.

1. Combine tequila alternative, lime juice, and black currant concentrate in a cocktail shaker.

2. Add large cubes of ice, cover the shaker, and shake vigorously 12–15 seconds. This mocktail is shaken for a bit longer since it includes a concentrate and you want that fully incorporated into the drink. The extra dilution helps as well.

3. Fill a Collins glass 2/3 full with ice cubes.

4. Strain the mixture into the glass.

5. Top with ginger beer.

6. Garnish with lime wheel.

Spicy Pineapple Margarita

Spicy margaritas are the perfect introduction to mocktails as they are relatively easy to make and taste very close to the real thing. This version uses jalapeño slices for the heat, which is balanced out by the lime juice, orange-infused simple syrup, and pineapple juice. Chili-lime seasoning is used on the rim to give the drink a nice pop of color, an extra kick, and a nice spicy aroma.

SERVES 1

Ingredients

1 tablespoon chili-lime seasoning for glass rim

1 lime wedge for glass rim

1 jalapeño slice

1 ounce lime juice

1 ounce Orange Simple Syrup (see recipe in Chapter 1)

2 ounces tequila alternative

2 ounces pineapple juice

1 small pineapple wedge and 1 jalapeño slice for garnish

Mocktail Twist

If you need a more subtle spice, skip the muddling step and just let the jalapeño incorporate its flavors through the shaking. Or, if you'd like a spicier drink, add more jalapeño slices to the muddling step.

1. Place chili-lime seasoning on a small plate.

2. Wet half the rim of a rocks glass using lime wedge. Dip that wet part of the rim into the chili-lime seasoning. (Only partially rimming the glass gives you and your guests the option of enjoying the margarita with or without the chili-lime seasoning.) Set the glass aside.

3. In a cocktail shaker, add 1 jalapeño slice and lime juice. Muddle jalapeño and lime juice together.

4. Add Orange Simple Syrup, tequila alternative, and pineapple juice.

5. Add large cubes of ice, cover the shaker, and shake vigorously 10–12 seconds.

6. Using a fine-mesh strainer, double-strain the mixture into the chili-lime seasoning–rimmed glass. This removes any small bits of jalapeño, which can be important if you want to avoid spicy surprises in your mocktail.

7. Carefully add a few cubes of ice into the rocks glass and garnish with pineapple wedge and 1 jalapeño slice on a cocktail pick.

Watermelon Margarita

The fresh watermelon juice is the star of this drink. It takes a bit of an effort to get fresh watermelon juice, but the effort is worth it. No juicer? No problem! You can blend chunks of watermelon in a food processor, then strain out the pulp using a fine-mesh strainer. If you have Orange Simple Syrup available, this would be a great alternative to the Simple Syrup and will add orange flavors to the drink.

SERVES 1

Ingredients

1 tablespoon sea salt for glass rim

1 teaspoon chili-lime seasoning for glass rim

1 lime wedge for glass rim

4 ounces fresh watermelon juice

1 ounce lime juice

1 ounce Simple Syrup (see recipe in Chapter 1)

2 ounces tequila alternative

1 small watermelon slice for garnish

Mocktail Twist

The chili-lime salt and watermelon combo is a popular one and for a good reason! The spiciness of the chili-lime makes the watermelon taste sweeter. Tajín is a popular brand of chili-lime seasoning that was invented in 1985 by Horacio Fernández Castillo.

1. Combine salt and chili-lime seasoning on a small plate.

2. Wet half the rim of a margarita glass using lime wedge.

3. Dip the wet part of the rim in salt and chili-lime mixture on the plate. (Only partially rimming the glass gives you and your guests the option to enjoy your margarita with or without the chili-lime seasoning.) Set the margarita glass aside.

4. In a cocktail shaker, combine watermelon juice, lime juice, Simple Syrup, and tequila alternative.

5. Add large cubes of ice, cover the shaker, and shake vigorously 10–12 seconds.

6. Strain the mixture into the chili-lime salt–rimmed margarita glass. Carefully add a few cubes of ice into the glass.

7. Finally, slice a notch at the tip of watermelon slice, and at the notch, place it on the rim of the margarita glass.

Cucumber Basil Margarita

This is one of the most refreshing margarita mocktails.
The cucumber and basil combination is herbaceous and crisp. This mocktail goes
very well with the agave flavors of the tequila alternative and leaves a peppery finish.
Finally, the tropical sweetness of the pineapple juice rounds out all the flavors.

SERVES 1

Ingredients

1 tablespoon sea salt for glass rim

1 lime wedge for glass rim

$1/3$ cup chopped unpeeled cucumber

$1/4$ ounce agave nectar

1 ounce lime juice

8 basil leaves

$1^1/2$ ounces tequila alternative

2 ounces pineapple juice

1 cucumber ribbon for garnish (see instructions in Chapter 1)

2–3 basil leaves or 1 small sprig of basil leaves for garnish

Mocktail Twist

Make cucumber ribbons by using a vegetable peeler and peeling a cucumber's full length. You can also turn the cucumber ribbon into a "rose" by grabbing one end of the cucumber ribbon with tongs to hold it in place and wrapping the ribbon in on itself in a circular motion.

1. Place salt on a small plate.

2. Wet half the rim of a margarita glass using lime wedge. Dip that wet part of the rim in salt. Set the margarita glass aside.

3. Combine cucumber chunks, agave nectar, and lime juice in a cocktail shaker.

4. Muddle cucumber and liquids together until well combined.

5. Tear 8 basil leaves in half and drop into the shaker.

6. Add tequila alternative and pineapple juice.

7. Add large cubes of ice, cover the shaker, and shake 12–15 seconds. This ensures that all ingredients are well combined while also slightly diluting the drink.

8. Using a fine-mesh strainer, double-strain the mixture into the salt-rimmed margarita glass, then carefully add a few cubes of ice.

9. Garnish with cucumber ribbon on a cocktail pick. Then complete the drink by resting 2–3 basil leaves or a small sprig of basil leaves on top of the cucumber ribbon.

Paloma with a Twist

This mocktail draws inspiration from Mexico's most popular
tequila-based cocktail—the Paloma. This mocktail uses fresh grapefruit juice and
tonic water in place of the standard grapefruit soda, and rosemary syrup is used to
add herbal notes. Diet tonic water can also be used as a substitute for a lower-calorie
option. The tequila alternative brings in agave flavors with a peppery finish that
simulates the burn of alcohol.

SERVES 1

Ingredients

2 ounces tequila alternative

2 ounces grapefruit juice

½ ounce lime juice

½ ounce rosemary syrup
(see Herb-Infused Simple
Syrup recipe in Chapter 1)

3 ounces tonic water

1 grapefruit slice and 1 rosemary
sprig for garnish

Mocktail Twist

This mocktail, the Paloma, is
believed to have been inspired
by and named after "La Paloma"
("The Dove"), which is a popular
folk song originating from the
early 1860s.

1. Combine tequila alternative, grapefruit juice, lime juice, and rosemary syrup in a cocktail shaker.

2. Add large cubes of ice, cover the shaker, and shake 10–12 seconds. Shaking the ingredients with ice not only chills and dilutes the drink but it also tames the tartness of the lime.

3. Fill a highball glass ⅔ full with ice cubes.

4. Strain the mixture into the glass.

5. Top with tonic water.

6. Garnish with grapefruit slice and rosemary sprig.

Coconut Margarita

The combination of coconut and lime works wonders in mocktails. This particular margarita is served "up." This means that it is shaken with ice and served in a coupe glass without ice. This gives the drink more concentrated flavors and less dilution. A margarita that's served up also looks visually appealing, even elegant.

SERVES 1

Ingredients

1 tablespoon cream of coconut for glass rim

1 tablespoon shredded sweetened coconut for glass rim

2 ounces tequila alternative

1 ounce coconut water

½ ounce lime juice

1 ounce cream of coconut

Mocktail Twist

Coconut cream and cream of coconut are two different products. Coconut cream is a thick and creamy liquid extracted from the flesh of mature coconuts. Cream of coconut is a sweetened coconut product made by blending coconut cream with sugar or other sweeteners.

1. Place 1 tablespoon cream of coconut on a small plate. On a separate small plate, add shredded coconut.

2. Wet half the rim of a coupe glass by dipping it in the plate with cream of coconut. Then dip that wet part of the rim in shredded coconut. Place coupe glass in the freezer to chill.

3. Combine tequila alternative, coconut water, lime juice, and 1 ounce cream of coconut in a cocktail shaker.

4. Add large cubes of ice, cover the shaker, and shake vigorously 10–12 seconds.

5. Using a fine-mesh strainer, double-strain the mixture into the chilled, coconut-rimmed coupe glass.

Jack Frost

You probably have seen a blue cocktail at least once in your life.
This blue color usually comes from blue curaçao liqueur, which is a sweet
and citrusy spirit. This mocktail uses a blue curaçao syrup that doesn't contain
alcohol. Only a little bit of the blue syrup is used to give it a very
light blue color. For a lower-calorie option, you can also substitute the
lemon-lime soda with a zero-sugar version.

SERVES 2

Ingredients

2 ounces tequila alternative

1 ounce nonalcoholic blue
curaçao syrup

2 ounces Low-Calorie Lemonade
(see recipe in Chapter 1)

3 ounces lemon-lime soda

1 cup regular ice cubes

1 tablespoon granulated sugar
for glass rim

1 teaspoon Simple Syrup
(see recipe in Chapter 1) for
glass rim

Mocktail Twist

The rise of blue cocktails is fairly
recent. They gained popularity
during the latter half of the
twentieth century. Blue curaçao
is typically used in cocktails and
mocktails with citrus or tropical
flavors.

1. Place two coupe glasses in the freezer, allowing
   them to chill as you prepare the mocktail.

2. In a blender, add tequila alternative, blue curaçao
   syrup, lemonade, and lemon-lime soda.

3. Add in ice. Cover and blend until smooth.

4. Place sugar on a small plate. Place Simple Syrup on
   a separate small plate. Take coupe glasses out of
   the freezer. Wet the rim of each glass by dipping it in
   Simple Syrup. Then dip the wet part into sugar.

5. Pour blended drink into the chilled, sugar-rimmed
   coupe glasses.

The Classic Margarita

Sometimes one just needs a classic margarita that is tart, sweet, and simple. To make a classic margarita mocktail, start with fresh ingredients and avoid using those sweet-and-sour mix bottles! You actually don't need those to make a classic margarita.

SERVES 1

Ingredients

1 tablespoon sea salt for glass rim

1 lime wedge for glass rim

2 ounces tequila alternative

1 ounce Orange Simple Syrup (see recipe in Chapter 1)

1 ounce lime juice

1 lime wheel for garnish

Mocktail Twist

This chapter covers many different approaches to the margarita, and we have only scratched the surface. You can really get creative with margaritas by combining different flavors, serving it iced or frozen, or even serving it up. The tequila alternative injects some complexity into the drink, and complexity is part of what makes a good mocktail good.

1. Place salt on a small plate.

2. Wet half the rim of a rocks glass or margarita glass using a lime wedge. Dip that wet part of the rim into salt. (Only partially rimming the glass gives you and your guests the option to enjoy the margarita with or without the salt.) Set the rocks glass or margarita glass aside.

3. In a cocktail shaker, combine tequila alternative, Orange Simple Syrup, and lime juice.

4. Add large cubes of ice, cover the shaker, and shake 10–12 seconds.

5. Strain the mixture into the salt-rimmed rocks glass or margarita glass.

6. Carefully add a few ice cubes, then garnish with lime wheel.

Tequila Espresso Martini

An intriguing flavor pairing, this mocktail combines the rich, bold flavors of coffee with the earthiness of the tequila alternative. It achieves a harmonious balance between the smoothness of espresso and fieriness of tequila alternative. To round out the flavors, citrus oils from orange peels are incorporated to brighten up the drink.

SERVES 1

Ingredients

2 ounces tequila alternative

1½ ounces Nonalcoholic Coffee Liqueur (see recipe in Chapter 1)

1½ ounces chilled espresso

½ ounce Simple Syrup (see recipe in Chapter 1)

2 pieces orange peel, divided

Mocktail Twist

Crema is the delicate layer of foam on top of a shot of espresso. This recipe also produces a crema thanks to the oil from the coffee beans in the espresso, giving the espresso martini its creamy or velvety texture.

1. Place a coupe glass in the freezer, allowing it to chill while you prepare the drink.

2. In a cocktail shaker, combine tequila alternative, coffee liqueur, espresso, and Simple Syrup.

3. Drop 1 orange peel into the shaker.

4. Add large cubes of ice, cover the shaker, and regal shake vigorously 10–12 seconds. Regal shaking (see Chapter 1) incorporates the citrus oils and slight bitterness from the pith into the drink. This step also allows the natural oils from the espresso to produce a nice foam.

5. Using a fine-mesh strainer, double-strain the mixture into the chilled coupe glass.

6. Use second orange peel to express some citrus oils on top of the drink by squeezing the pith side of the peel toward the top of the drink so the oils spray into it. This gives a nice aroma while the mocktail is sipped.

7. Finally, garnish with the same orange peel, either placed on the rim of the glass or dropped into the drink.

CHAPTER 5

WHISKEY-INSPIRED MOCKTAILS

Inspired by the flavor profile of whiskey, most alternatives on the market highlight notes of oak, vanilla, and caramel. Some of them are smoky and some mimic the alcohol burn with a peppery finish at the end.

When designing cocktails, you want to incorporate ingredients that all work together without one flavor overpowering the other. Whiskey works well with fruits like orange, cherry, and pineapple to add freshness to the drink. Using sweeteners that complement whiskey's vanilla flavors, like demerara syrup or maple syrup, is another way of packing in flavor without adding extra volume to the cocktail. Lemon juice adds just the right amount of acidity without throwing off the balance of the drink.

Pulling inspiration from classic recipes like the old-fashioned and from everyday ingredients like fig orange spread, this chapter features summer drink recipes as well as some that are more suited for fall and winter.

Maple Old-Fashioned

This mocktail draws inspiration from the timeless old-fashioned. Instead of using sugar and dissolving it with water, this version uses bourbon barrel–aged maple syrup. This enhances the notes of oak and vanilla that come from the nonalcoholic bourbon. It also adds a nice texture to the drink. If you like, place a cinnamon stick in the finished drink as an extra garnish.

SERVES 1

Ingredients

2 ounces nonalcoholic bourbon

1 teaspoon bourbon barrel–aged maple syrup

4 dashes alcohol-free aromatic bitters

1 orange peel and 1 maraschino cherry for garnish

Mocktail Twist

Angostura bitters can also be used if you're comfortable with trace amounts of alcohol. Depending on volume used, usually 1–2 dashes, the drink can still be considered nonalcoholic even when using alcoholic bitters.

1. Place your mixing glass in the freezer, allowing it to chill as you gather and prepare the other ingredients.

2. When ready, take out the mixing glass from the freezer and in it combine nonalcoholic bourbon, maple syrup, and bitters.

3. Add large cubes of ice so that the mixing glass is two-thirds full.

4. Using a bar spoon, stir so that the spoon slowly circles around the glass in a manner that gets the ice to rotate as well. Stir about 30 seconds.

5. Put a big cube of ice into a rocks glass. Place a Julep or Hawthorne strainer over the mixing glass. Strain the mixture into the rocks glass.

6. Express orange oil from orange peel over the drink. Do this by squeezing the pith side of the peel toward the top of the drink so the oils spray into it.

7. Finally, garnish with orange peel and cherry on a cocktail pick.

The FOG (Fig Orange Ginger)

Whether a cocktail or a mocktail, one critical element of the drink
is texture. In this mocktail, the texture is enhanced by the fig orange spread.
The right amount of spread adds a subtle sweetness and, in this case, fig and
orange flavors into the drink. Orange goes really well with the oaky,
vanilla notes of the whiskey alternative.

SERVES 1

Ingredients

2 ounces whiskey alternative

3 dashes alcohol-free orange
  bitters

$\frac{1}{2}$ ounce lime juice

$\frac{1}{2}$ tablespoon fig orange spread

4 ounces ginger beer

1 dehydrated orange wheel and
  1 basil leaf for garnish

Mocktail Twist

There are many unique flavor
combinations in spreads and
jams these days! Consider using
them in place of syrup in your
next mocktail for expanded flavor
possibilities!

1. In a cocktail shaker, combine whiskey alternative, bitters, lime juice, and fig orange spread.

2. Add large cubes of ice, cover the shaker, and shake vigorously 12–15 seconds. Shaking it a bit longer than usual makes sure that the fig orange spread is well incorporated into the drink.

3. Fill a highball glass $\frac{2}{3}$ full with ice cubes.

4. Using a fine-mesh strainer, double-strain the mixture into the glass. This step effectively filters out any remnants of the fig orange spread including fig seeds, which might be unpleasant in the drink.

5. Top with ginger beer.

6. Finally, garnish with orange wheel and basil. To make it more visually appealing, attach garnishes to one side of the glass using a mini clothespin.

Cherry Almond Sour

The pairing of cherry and almond is a good flavor combination for mocktails. This recipe uses the combination of tart cherry juice and orgeat syrup. Orgeat syrup is a sweetener made from almonds and available in most liquor stores or online. This is the perfect drink to sip on as you unwind after a long day.

SERVES 1

Ingredients

1½ ounces whiskey alternative

2 ounces tart cherry juice

½ ounce lime juice

¾ ounce orgeat syrup

1 lime peel and 1 maraschino cherry for garnish

Mocktail Twist

Orgeat syrup is made from almonds, sugar, and either rose water or orange blossom water. It is a key ingredient in many tiki drinks, with mai tai being one of the more popular ones.

1. In a cocktail shaker, combine whiskey alternative, tart cherry juice, lime juice, and orgeat syrup.

2. Add large cubes of ice, cover the shaker, and shake 10–12 seconds. This step not only chills the drink but also makes sure that the orgeat syrup, which is somewhat thick in consistency, is well incorporated into the drink.

3. Put a big cube of ice into a rocks glass.

4. Strain the mixture into the glass.

5. Finally, garnish with lime peel and cherry. For an extra flair, make a citrus flag garnish by wrapping lime wheel around cherry and piercing it with a cocktail pick.

Highland Mule

This mocktail version of the Moscow mule uses a whiskey alternative as the base spirit, which adds depth to the drink while incorporating notes of oak and vanilla. Another key ingredient in any mule is the ginger beer, so it is important to select a good quality ginger beer for this drink. It is best to serve this drink in a copper mug; however, if one is not available, a highball glass will work.

SERVES 1

Ingredients

2 ounces whiskey alternative

½ ounce lime juice

4 ounces ginger beer

1 dehydrated lime wheel and 2–3 mint sprigs for garnish

Mocktail Twist

There are many variations of the popular Moscow mule. They can be made by switching the traditional base spirit (vodka) with a different spirit. The possibilities are many: Jamaican mule (spiced rum), Mexican mule (tequila), London mule (gin), the list goes on. If you prefer a more subtle ginger flavor, ginger ale can be used in place of ginger beer. There are also light ginger beer options for a lower-calorie version of this drink.

1. In a copper mug or highball glass, add whiskey alternative and lime juice.

2. Top it off with ginger beer and give it a light stir.

3. Fill the mug or glass with crushed ice using a scoop or a spoon and garnish it by resting lime wheel on the glass rim. Lastly, create a mint bouquet by twisting together mint sprigs. Give mint a light slap on the palm of your hand, and place it on top of the drink.

Whiskey Business

A beautiful drink with a dark red hue, this mocktail combines the tartness
of the homemade lemonade and smokiness of the whiskey alternative, finished
off with a splash of cranberry juice that adds just a hint of sweetness and
bitterness. Since a significant component of this mocktail is the lemonade,
using fresh lemonade makes a big difference in the flavor.

SERVES 1

Ingredients

1 ounce whiskey alternative

3 ounces Low-Calorie Lemonade
(see recipe in Chapter 1)

1 ounce cranberry juice

1 lemon twist for garnish

Mocktail Twist

Make a lemon twist by wrapping
a lemon peel tightly around a
chopstick. If available, use small
clothespins (available at craft
stores) to affix both ends of the
lemon peel to the chopstick. By
the time you're done making the
drink, the lemon twist will hold
its shape.

1. In a cocktail shaker, combine whiskey alternative,
lemonade, and juice.

2. Add large cubes of ice, cover the shaker, and shake
vigorously 10–12 seconds or until the exterior of the
shaker gets visibly frosty.

3. Put a big cube of ice in a rocks glass. Strain the
mixture into the glass.

4. Finally, garnish with lemon twist.

Dr. Fleming

This mocktail is inspired by the cocktail called Penicillin, created by a bartender named Sam Ross. The original recipe combines the smoky flavors of Scotch whisky and the spicy notes of ginger. In this mocktail version, a smoky whiskey alternative is sweetened by Honey Syrup, brightened by lemon juice, and finished with the fiery flavors of ginger via the Ginger Shot.

SERVES 1

Ingredients

2 ounces whiskey alternative

½ ounce Ginger Shot (see recipe in Chapter 1)

¾ ounce Honey Syrup (see recipe in Chapter 1)

¾ ounce lemon juice

1 slice unpeeled ginger root or 1 piece candied ginger for garnish

Mocktail Twist

Ginger shots are also available in most grocery stores in the US. The shots often include lemon juice, so you can adjust the lemon juice in this or any mocktail recipe as necessary. Ginger shots work great in mocktails not just because of their strong flavor but also because of their health benefits. It's a solid mocktail recipe that's easy to make and also packed with nutrients!

1. In a cocktail shaker, combine whiskey alternative, Ginger Shot, Honey Syrup, and lemon juice.

2. Add large cubes of ice, cover the shaker, and shake vigorously 10–12 seconds or until the exterior of the shaker gets visibly frosty.

3. Put a big cube of ice in a rocks glass. Strain the mixture into the glass.

4. Garnish with ginger root or candied ginger on a cocktail pick.

Whiskey Sidecar

The traditional sidecar cocktail is made with cognac but unfortunately there's no available nonalcoholic cognac alternative yet. In this Whiskey Sidecar mocktail, whiskey alternative is used in place of the cognac. An orange-infused simple syrup and a few dashes of orange bitters are also added to incorporate citrus flavors into the drink.

SERVES 1

Ingredients

2 ounces whiskey alternative

1 ounce Orange Simple Syrup (see recipe in Chapter 1)

1 ounce lemon juice

3 dashes alcohol-free orange bitters

1 orange peel for garnish

Mocktail Twist

The sidecar is based on the "sour" family of cocktails, like the daiquiri. This mocktail version actually resembles other sours more than the alcoholic sidecar, because the syrup is swapped in for the liqueur to make it a little sweeter.

1. Place a martini glass in the freezer, allowing it to chill as you prepare the mocktail.

2. In a cocktail shaker, combine whiskey alternative, Orange Simple Syrup, lemon juice, and bitters.

3. Add large cubes of ice, cover the shaker, and shake vigorously 10–12 seconds or until the exterior of the shaker becomes visibly frosty.

4. Using a fine-mesh strainer, double-strain the mixture into the chilled martini glass, effectively removing any small ice fragments for a smooth and refined mocktail.

5. Finally, skewer orange peel with a cocktail pick and rest this on top of the martini glass for garnish.

Pineapple Cinnamon Whiskey Sour

This mocktail is inspired by the popular Brazilian dessert called "abacaxi com canela," which means "pineapple with cinnamon." This recipe mixes the combination of pineapple and cinnamon with a whiskey alternative that provides notes of vanilla and caramel. The addition of egg white provides a smooth, velvety texture that is a nice introduction to this mocktail when you first take a sip.

SERVES 1

Ingredients

2 ounces whiskey alternative

$3/4$ ounce lemon juice

$1/2$ ounce pineapple juice

$1/2$ ounce demerara syrup (see Simple Syrup recipe in Chapter 1)

1 dash ground cinnamon

$3/4$ ounce egg white

1 pineapple frond and 1 dash ground cinnamon for garnish

Mocktail Twist

Whiskey and demerara syrup work well together. The flavors of molasses from the demerara syrup accentuate the smoky vanilla taste that is typical in most nonalcoholic whiskeys.

1. Place a Nick and Nora glass in the freezer, allowing it to chill as you prepare the mocktail.

2. Combine whiskey alternative, lemon juice, pineapple juice, demerara syrup, and dash of cinnamon in a cocktail shaker.

3. Using a jigger, measure $3/4$ ounce egg white and add that to the shaker. (Depending on the size of the egg, sometimes including all the egg white produces too much foam, so it is best to measure the egg white.)

4. Without adding any ice, cover the shaker and dry shake vigorously for 20 seconds.

5. Add ice to the shaker, cover, and wet shake another 10 seconds.

6. Using a fine-mesh strainer, double-strain the mixture into the chilled Nick and Nora glass.

7. Garnish with pineapple frond and then add a dash of cinnamon.

Orange Basil Smash

This is a refreshing mocktail that has a pronounced citrus flavor, a touch of sweetness, herbal notes from the basil, and a subtle depth from the nonalcoholic whiskey. Muddling the orange wedges releases their aromatic oils into the drink and intensifies the citrus flavor while also incorporating a little bitterness into it.

SERVES 1

Ingredients

2 orange wedges ($\frac{1}{8}$ of a whole medium orange)

1 ounce fresh orange juice

$\frac{1}{2}$ ounce lemon juice

$\frac{1}{4}$ ounce Simple Syrup (see recipe in Chapter 1)

4 basil leaves

2 ounces whiskey alternative

1 orange peel and 1 basil leaf for garnish

Mocktail Twist

Muddling oranges with the rind and skin adds a layer of bitterness to mocktails. It also incorporates citrus oils into the drink, which provides a good aroma.

1. In a cocktail shaker, add orange wedges, orange juice, lemon juice, and Simple Syrup.

2. Using a muddler or the back of a wooden spoon, muddle until oranges are broken into small pieces and the citrus oils from the peels are extracted.

3. Tear 4 basil leaves in half and drop them into the cocktail shaker.

4. Add whiskey alternative, then add large cubes of ice.

5. Cover the shaker and shake vigorously 10–12 seconds.

6. Using a fine-mesh strainer, double-strain the mixture into a rocks glass. This step effectively filters out any remnants of muddled oranges and basil leaves.

7. Finally, garnish with orange peel and 1 basil leaf.

Irish Coffee

This mocktail uses a whiskey alternative to mimic the delightful kick of Irish whiskey. It is combined with coffee and sweetened by brown sugar. The foam on top is creamy with a touch of vanilla sweetness. It's perfect for when you want something that wakes you up while still feeling that you're having a proper drink.

SERVES 1

Ingredients

Vanilla Foam

⅛ cup heavy cream
½ teaspoon vanilla syrup

Irish Coffee

1½ ounces whiskey alternative
5 ounces hot brewed coffee
1 teaspoon brown sugar

Mocktail Twist

The history of Irish coffee started in an Irish airport where passengers usually face long flights with adverse weather conditions. A chef named Joe Sheridan whipped up this warm and comforting drink for some waiting passengers and it became an instant hit. If you want to enjoy this drink later in the day or after a nice dinner, you can use decaffeinated coffee so you can still enjoy this hot drink without worrying about insomnia later.

1. Using a whisk or a frother, make Vanilla Foam in a small mixing bowl by lightly whipping together cream and vanilla syrup until the cream is slightly thickened, then set aside.

2. In an Irish coffee mug or a clear glass mug, add whiskey alternative and coffee.

3. Stir in sugar until fully dissolved.

4. Top with Vanilla Foam by pouring it on top of the drink or by using a spoon.

Irish Cream

This mocktail can be enjoyed on its own or over ice, or it can be used as an ingredient to make other mocktails or cocktails. You can even use it in place of a creamer with your black coffee, which will sweeten it while adding unique flavors from the whiskey alternative.

SERVES 2

Ingredients

1/2 cup whiskey alternative

1/4 cup heavy cream

1/2 tablespoon chocolate syrup

1/4 teaspoon instant coffee

1/4 (14-ounce) can sweetened condensed milk

2 chocolate balls for garnish

Mocktail Twist

The most popular brand of (alcoholic) Irish cream is Baileys. As with that alcoholic cousin, this mocktail can be enjoyed cold or hot, or used as an ingredient to make another mocktail.

1. In a mixing glass, combine whiskey alternative, cream, chocolate syrup, coffee, and condensed milk.

2. Using a whisk or a frother, mix until ingredients are well combined. Since the condensed milk is thick, it will take a little bit of time to fully incorporate it with the other ingredients.

3. Add a few ice cubes to two rocks glasses. Pour the smooth mixture into the glasses.

4. Garnish each drink with 1 chocolate ball on a cocktail pick.

CHAPTER 6

WINE-INSPIRED MOCKTAILS

While wines are meant to be sipped and enjoyed as they are, wines can also be used in mocktails to add a layer of depth and complexity to the concoctions. There are many uses for wine in mocktails. They can be the star of the show or a supporting cast member, helping to lift the flavors of the other ingredients. Sparkling wines add texture and unique flavors to mocktails. Most dealcoholized sparkling wines available on the market taste really close to the real thing, which allows for great creativity with champagne cocktails like the French 75 and various spritzes and mimosas. Nonalcoholic white wines and red wines are perfect for sangrias or other drinks with fresh fruit flavors and carbonation, for a refreshing summer punch. From mimosas to Bellinis and sangrias, you'll find something that you can make with nonalcoholic wines and other simple ingredients that are easy to find.

Apple Ginger White Sangria

This recipe is especially simple because it uses just one type of fruit: apples. Most dealcoholized sauvignon blanc options already have citrus flavors and some acidity in them, so one need not include fresh citrus fruits. But feel free to add oranges or lemons if you have them on hand and you prefer a more citrusy sangria.

SERVES 1

Ingredients

1 small unpeeled apple, cored and cut into $\frac{1}{2}$" chunks

4 ounces nonalcoholic sauvignon blanc

2 ounces apple cider

$\frac{1}{2}$ ounce ginger syrup

1 apple fan for garnish (see instructions in Chapter 1)

Mocktail Twist

Sangrias are very easy to make, and now that there are many dealcoholized wine options on the market, nonalcoholic sangrias have the potential to taste just as complex as their alcoholic counterparts. This recipe can even be scaled up to make a pitcherful of sangria so that you can impress your guests. To do this, just mix all ingredients (scaled up) in a big pitcher, refrigerate, then add ice just before serving.

1. Add $\frac{1}{4}$ cup apple chunks to a stemless wine glass. (You can add more apple if desired, or reserve the rest for another use.)

2. Add nonalcoholic sauvignon blanc, cider, and ginger syrup.

3. Stir to combine all ingredients.

4. Carefully add a few cubes of ice into the glass.

5. Garnish with apple fan.

Strawberry Basil Mimosa

This Strawberry Basil Mimosa combines fresh strawberries and basil leaves with alcohol-removed sparkling rosé. The dealcoholized bubbly adds texture and a layer of depth that makes the drink taste like a proper adult beverage.

SERVES 1

Ingredients

- 4 medium strawberries, chopped into quarters
- $1/2$ ounce lemon juice
- 1 ounce Simple Syrup (see recipe in Chapter 1)
- 6 basil leaves
- 5 ounces alcohol-removed sparkling rosé
- 1 small strawberry and 2 basil leaves for garnish

Mocktail Twist

This recipe can be made using one of two methods: shaken and strained, or simply built right in the glass. To build this drink directly in the glass, choose a stemless wine glass and gently muddle the ingredients, top with the alcohol-removed sparkling rosé, fill it with ice, and give it a nice stir. Note: Never muddle in a stemmed wine glass because they are easy to break!

1. In a cocktail shaker, add chopped strawberries, lemon juice, Simple Syrup, and 6 basil leaves.

2. Using a muddler or a wooden spoon, muddle the ingredients together until strawberries are broken into very small pieces.

3. Add large cubes of ice to the shaker, cover it, and shake vigorously 10–12 seconds or until the exterior of the shaker becomes visibly frosty.

4. Fill a stemless wine glass $2/3$ full with ice cubes.

5. Strain the mixture into the glass. You can also use a fine-mesh strainer if you don't want any remnants of muddled fruit in your drink.

6. Top with alcohol-removed sparkling rosé.

7. Garnish with strawberry and 2 basil leaves.

Bellini

The original Bellini recipe calls for white peach purée and prosecco. While using fresh fruits in mocktails is generally the best way to go, you can sometimes substitute canned fruit, as this recipe does. If making this recipe with fresh peaches, choose peaches that are very ripe, and substitute $1/2$ ounce simple syrup for the syrup from the canned peaches.

SERVES 2

Ingredients

Peach Purée

2 peach halves, canned in heavy syrup

$1/2$ ounce heavy syrup from the canned peaches

Nonalcoholic Bellini

4 ounces Peach Purée

8 ounces chilled nonalcoholic sparkling brut

Mocktail Twist

Using canned peaches has the advantage of making the Peach Purée smoother and silkier than with fresh peaches. If using fresh peaches, however, selecting very ripe peaches and adding simple syrup will help the purée achieve a nice consistency. Frozen peaches can also be used. Thaw the frozen peaches first and treat them like fresh peaches in the recipe.

1. Make Peach Purée by placing peach halves and syrup into a food processor or a blender and blending until you get a smooth consistency. Put purée in the refrigerator to chill at least 30 minutes.

2. When Peach Purée is chilled, pour 2 ounces purée into each of two champagne flutes.

3. To finish making Bellini, fill each champagne flute with 4 ounces nonalcoholic sparkling brut. Do this carefully and slowly to prevent it from fizzing over.

4. Gently stir the mixture with a bar spoon or a regular spoon to combine the ingredients.

Bubbly Berry Lavender

This drink is similar to a Bellini except it uses berries and has a floral touch, which is perfect if you don't like peaches. This recipe will also allow you to experiment with different variations of the drink. Use whatever berries you have in your refrigerator and mix them with a simple syrup to make a purée. With this recipe as a template, you can build a bubbly mocktail of your choosing.

SERVES 2

Ingredients

Berry Lavender Purée

3 medium strawberries

¼ cup blueberries

½ ounce Lavender Simple Syrup (see recipe in Chapter 1)

Bubbly Berry Lavender

4 ounces Berry Lavender Purée

8 ounces chilled nonalcoholic sparkling brut

1 medium strawberry, cut in half, and 2–3 blueberries for garnish

Mocktail Twist

If you don't have time to make your own floral or herbal syrup, these can be purchased online as well. Some liquor stores also carry different kinds of simple syrups.

1. Make Berry Lavender Purée by placing berries and Lavender Simple Syrup into a food processor or a blender and blending until you get a smooth consistency. Put the purée in the refrigerator to chill at least 30 minutes.

2. When Berry Lavender Purée is chilled, pour 2 ounces purée into each of two champagne flutes.

3. To make Bubbly Berry Lavender, fill each champagne flute with 4 ounces nonalcoholic sparkling brut. Do this carefully and slowly to prevent it from fizzing over.

4. Gently stir the mixture with a bar spoon or a regular spoon to combine the ingredients.

5. Finally, skewer strawberry pieces and blueberries on two cocktail picks and use these to garnish the champagne flutes.

French 75

Inspired by the classic French 75, this mocktail uses juniper berries to infuse piney flavors into the drink, mimicking the flavor of gin. A few dashes of orange bitters are also added to help bind the juniper flavors to the rest of the ingredients. Mix in bright and tart lemon juice, a touch of sweetness, and nonalcoholic sparkling brut, and you have a sophisticated mocktail in your hands.

SERVES 1

Ingredients

1/2 ounce lemon juice

1/2 ounce Juniper Simple Syrup (see recipe in Chapter 1)

7 dried juniper berries

4 dashes alcohol-free orange bitters

4 ounces nonalcoholic sparkling brut

1 lemon twist for garnish

Mocktail Twist

If you do have a gin alternative available, you can skip the juniper berries in this recipe and add 11/2 ounces gin alternative. This will give the mocktail a nice kick since most gin alternatives have a peppery finish in them to simulate the alcohol burn. Since this nonalcoholic cocktail is essentially a champagne cocktail, you can also serve it in champagne flutes.

1. Place a coupe glass in the freezer, allowing it to chill as you prepare the mocktail.

2. In a cocktail shaker, combine lemon juice, Juniper Simple Syrup, berries, and bitters.

3. Add large cubes of ice, cover the shaker, and shake vigorously 12–15 seconds or until the exterior of the shaker becomes visibly frosty.

4. To achieve a smooth texture, double-strain the mixture into the chilled coupe glass using a fine-mesh strainer, effectively removing any small ice fragments and any remnants of berries.

5. Finally, top with nonalcoholic sparkling brut and garnish with lemon twist.

Rosemary Citrus Fizz

This mocktail has a unique blend of bright and bitter citrus flavors, thanks to the strength of the grapefruit and the herbal depth of the rosemary. In this recipe, the rosemary sprig is added to the shaker just before shaking. This method is similar to "regal shaking" in which a citrus peel is added directly in the shaker prior to shaking. Including the rosemary breaks down the herb, allowing the release of its oils, which are then incorporated into the drink.

SERVES 1

Ingredients

2 ounces grapefruit juice

$1/2$ ounce lemon juice

$1/2$ ounce Simple Syrup
(see recipe in Chapter 1)

2 rosemary sprigs, divided
(1 for garnish)

4 ounces chilled nonalcoholic
sparkling brut

Mocktail Twist

This mocktail can also be served in a coupe glass. Make sure to put the coupe glass in the freezer to allow it to chill while you make the drink.

1. In a cocktail shaker, combine grapefruit juice, lemon juice, and Simple Syrup.

2. Put 1 rosemary sprig into the shaker.

3. Add large cubes of ice, cover the shaker, and shake vigorously 10–12 seconds or until the exterior of the shaker becomes visibly frosty.

4. Using a fine-mesh strainer, double-strain the mixture into a champagne flute. This effectively filters out any remnants of rosemary sprig and any small ice fragments.

5. Top with nonalcoholic sparkling brut.

6. Lightly stir to combine all ingredients.

7. Finally, garnish with the remaining rosemary sprig.

Cherry Vanilla Blush

This champagne cocktail is very easy to make because it is built
in the same glass you'll serve it in. The tart cherry juice's earthy flavor goes
well with vanilla, while the sparkling brut provides carbonation and texture
to this drink. Think of it as an elevated mimosa.

SERVES 1

Ingredients

1¾ ounces tart cherry juice

½ ounce cherry syrup

½ teaspoon alcohol-free vanilla extract

4 ounces nonalcoholic sparkling brut

3 maraschino cherries for garnish

Mocktail Twist

Tart cherry juice is "having a moment" lately due to its potential health benefits. It naturally contains melatonin, which helps regulate the sleep cycle. It also has anti-inflammatory properties and is rich in antioxidants. The easiest way to get the needed cherry syrup for this drink is by using the syrup from a jar of regular maraschino cherries. Brands like Monin and Torani also sell cherry syrup.

1. In a large wine glass, add juice, cherry syrup, and vanilla.

2. Add a couple large cubes of ice and mix until the ingredients are combined.

3. Top with nonalcoholic sparkling brut and lightly stir.

4. Garnish with cherries skewered on a cocktail pick.

Calimocho

Inspired by the cocktail called Calimocho or Kalimotxo, this mocktail uses equal parts nonalcoholic red wine and cola. The cola's sweetness and texture work really well with the acidity of the nonalcoholic red wine. A few dashes of alcohol-free aromatic bitters or Angostura bitters rounds out the drink.

SERVES 1

Ingredients

- 3 ounces dealcoholized cabernet sauvignon
- 2 dashes alcohol-free aromatic bitters
- 3 ounces chilled cola
- $\frac{1}{4}$ ounce lemon juice
- 1 lemon twist for garnish

Mocktail Twist

Replicating the taste and texture of red wine, without alcohol, is hard to do. If you've been exploring the world of nonalcoholic beverages, there's a high likelihood that you've encountered a nonalcoholic red wine that's not good. If ever this happens again, use this recipe to make an enjoyable mocktail. If you have a rum alternative, add 1 ounce to this recipe for an extra kick and an elevated flavor profile!

1. Place a goblet or highball glass in the freezer to chill.
2. In the chilled glass, fill $\frac{2}{3}$ full with ice then pour in dealcoholized cabernet sauvignon.
3. Add 2 dashes of alcohol-free aromatic bitters then gently add cola and lemon juice.
4. Give it a light stir to combine.
5. Finally, garnish with lemon twist.

Red Sangria

If you're looking for a batch mocktail that's easy to make on a hot summer day when guests are over, look no further. This nonalcoholic take on a red sangria uses fresh fruits and dealcoholized red wine. The addition of ginger beer adds texture, a bit of spice, and a little sweetness.

SERVES 4

Ingredients

1 medium unpeeled orange, seeded and chopped in small pieces

1 medium unpeeled apple, sliced, cored, and chopped

1 medium unpeeled lemon, seeded and cut into wedges

1 (750-milliliter) bottle dealcoholized cabernet sauvignon

6 dashes alcohol-free aromatic bitters

$7\frac{1}{2}$ ounces ginger beer

1 medium orange for garnish

Mocktail Twist

The ginger beer can be substituted with ginger ale for a less spicy version. Fresh orange juice can also be added if a sweeter sangria is preferred.

1. Place chopped orange, apple, and lemon in a large pitcher.

2. With a muddler or the back of a wooden spoon, press into the fruits to extract their juices.

3. Pour in dealcoholized cabernet sauvignon.

4. Add bitters. Stir and refrigerate at least 1 hour.

5. Slice remaining orange into $\frac{1}{4}$"-thick orange wheels. Set these aside until ready to serve the drink (if not serving for a while, refrigerate orange wheels).

6. Just before serving, gently pour in ginger beer then lightly stir.

7. When you're ready to serve, add ice cubes to four wine glasses, pour in sangria while also including some of the muddled fruit in the glass, and then garnish each glass with 1 orange wheel.

Crimson Mimosa

This mocktail is a cross between a French 75 and a mimosa.
It uses fresh blood orange juice instead of gin (which makes it more like a
mimosa). It also uses Juniper Simple Syrup that mimics the flavor of gin (which
makes it more like a French 75). Regardless of how it's categorized, the important
thing is that this drink is delicious, and has a striking color.

SERVES 1

Ingredients

2 ounces fresh blood orange juice

½ ounce lemon juice

½ ounce Juniper Simple Syrup
(see recipe in Chapter 1)

4 ounces chilled nonalcoholic
sparkling brut

1 blood orange wedge for garnish

Mocktail Twist

Blood oranges are sometimes called raspberry oranges due to their raspberry-like flavor. Not only are they rich in vitamin C, but they also have antioxidants and anti-inflammatory properties!

1. Place a coupe glass in the freezer, ensuring it becomes chilled while you prepare the drink.

2. In a cocktail shaker, combine blood orange juice, lemon juice, and Juniper Simple Syrup.

3. Add large cubes of ice, cover the shaker, and shake vigorously 10–12 seconds or until the exterior of the shaker becomes visibly frosty. Shaking also softens the acidity of the citrus juices and helps aerate the drink for texture.

4. To achieve a smooth texture, double-strain the mixture into the chilled coupe glass using a fine-mesh strainer, effectively removing any small ice fragments.

5. Top with nonalcoholic sparkling brut.

6. Stir lightly, then garnish with blood orange wedge on the rim of the glass.

CHAPTER 7

APERITIFS

The word "aperitif" comes from the Latin word "aper-ire," which means "to open." Aperitifs are drinks that aim to stimulate your appetite before a meal. While there are many kinds of aperitifs, there are still only a handful of nonalcoholic options available in this category. This chapter focuses on nonalcoholic Italian bitter aperitifs that are either crimson or bright orange in color, since they are the most common aperitifs available without alcohol.

Most nonalcoholic aperitifs have a subtle sweetness to them, so you'll find that the recipes here only use a little bit of syrup, if at all, and then mostly for texture. Also, since aperitifs are bitter, most of the recipes have an ingredient that provides carbonation and dilution.

A curation of refreshing and effervescent mocktails that are meant to be sipped slowly, these drinks can be enjoyed as you unwind and socialize before dinner. Sit back and savor the flavors!

The New Shirley

The standard Shirley Temple recipe calls for ginger ale and a splash of grenadine. This version draws inspiration from the flavors of the original recipe. Fresh pomegranate seeds are used to replicate the pomegranate flavors of grenadine, ginger beer is used for a more pronounced ginger flavor, and a nonalcoholic Italian aperitif is used to give the drink a layer of citrus bitterness and depth.

SERVES 1

Ingredients

3 tablespoons pomegranate seeds

3 dashes alcohol-free orange bitters

1¼ ounces lemon juice

1½ ounces nonalcoholic Italian orange aperitif

4 ounces ginger beer

1 lemon peel and 1 cocktail cherry for garnish

Mocktail Twist

Ginger ale can also be used in place of ginger beer for a more subtle flavor. As in the original Shirley Temple, lemon-lime soda can also be used as a substitute for ginger beer.

1. Combine pomegranate seeds, bitters, and lemon juice in a cocktail shaker.

2. Using a muddler or the back of a wooden spoon, muddle the ingredients together, making sure that the juices are extracted from the pomegranate seeds.

3. Add nonalcoholic aperitif to the shaker.

4. Add large cubes of ice, cover the shaker, and shake vigorously 10–12 seconds or until the exterior of the shaker becomes visibly frosty.

5. Fill a highball glass ⅔ full with ice.

6. Using a fine-mesh strainer, double-strain the mixture into the glass.

7. Garnish with lemon peel and cocktail cherry on a cocktail pick.

Bitter Orange Sparkler

This nonalcoholic sparkler is inspired by the Aperol spritz,
which was created by bartender Raimondo Ricci in 1919. This mocktail
uses a nonalcoholic Italian orange aperitif. If that's not available in your area,
you'll probably have better luck with nonalcoholic Italian red aperitifs. If you choose
an Italian red aperitif as a substitute, use only $1\frac{1}{2}$ ounces because these are
usually more bitter. And if you don't have access to nonalcoholic sparkling
brut, a good quality tonic water will also work.

SERVES 1

Ingredients
- 2 ounces nonalcoholic Italian orange aperitif
- 1 ounce club soda
- 2 dashes alcohol-free orange bitters
- 3 ounces nonalcoholic sparkling brut
- 1 orange wedge for garnish

Mocktail Twist
Thankfully, there are a number of nonalcoholic Italian bitter aperitifs on the market now, so making a nonalcoholic version of this drink is easier. When mixing this mocktail, make sure to stir lightly so that the carbonation is preserved and you can enjoy the bubbles for longer. Enjoy this nonalcoholic sparkler as a predinner drink or sip it poolside!

1. Add large cubes of ice to a red wine glass, then add nonalcoholic aperitif, club soda, bitters, and nonalcoholic sparkling brut.
2. Lightly stir until ingredients are well combined.
3. Garnish with orange wedge inside the glass.

Italian Sparkler

This citrus-forward mocktail has just the right balance of sweet and bitter. This mocktail also uses Juniper Simple Syrup to give it a touch of piney flavor that mimics gin. If you do have a gin alternative on hand, add 1 1/2 ounces of that to give this mocktail a nice kick. Most gin alternatives have a peppery finish that mimics the alcohol burn.

SERVES 1

Ingredients

2 ounces nonalcoholic Italian red aperitif

1 ounce grapefruit juice

1/2 ounce Juniper Simple Syrup (see recipe in Chapter 1)

4 ounces tonic water

1 grapefruit wedge and 1 orange wedge for garnish

Mocktail Twist

For a lower-calorie option, you can use a zero-sugar tonic water. Club soda can also be used instead of tonic water for more carbonation and less bitterness. Regular simple syrup can also be used instead of the Juniper Simple Syrup.

1. In a cocktail shaker, combine nonalcoholic aperitif, juice, and Juniper Simple Syrup.

2. Add large cubes of ice, cover the shaker, and shake vigorously 10–12 seconds or until the exterior of the shaker becomes visibly frosty.

3. Fill a highball glass 2/3 full with ice cubes.

4. Strain the mixture into the glass, and top with tonic water.

5. Garnish with grapefruit and orange wedges. For a unique-looking citrus wedge garnish, add a slice mark to the wedge across the outer peel/pith part, and affix the wedge on the rim of the glass at the slice mark so that the citrus flesh is facing up.

Strawberry Negroni Smash

This mocktail is a refreshing twist on the Negroni cocktail.
Instead of replacing gin with another spirit alternative, it is replaced with
strawberries. The strawberries add freshness and a nice hue to the drink.
The Juniper Simple Syrup can be skipped if the strawberries are sweet
enough. To maintain the illusion that the drink contains gin, add 8 dried
juniper berries to the shaker just before shaking it with ice.

SERVES 1

Ingredients

- 3 medium strawberries
- 1 ounce lemon juice
- ¼ ounce Juniper Simple Syrup
  (see recipe in Chapter 1)
- 2 ounces nonalcoholic Italian red
  aperitif
- 1 strawberry slice for garnish

Mocktail Twist

There are numerous variations on
the classic Negroni cocktail. The
original recipe calls for Campari,
gin, and sweet red vermouth.
But replace the gin with bourbon
and you have the Boulevardier
cocktail. Replace the gin with
prosecco and you have the
Negroni Sbagliato. Replace the
gin with tequila and you have the
Rosita. The list goes on.

1. In a cocktail shaker, use a muddler or the back of
   a wooden spoon to muddle strawberries, lemon
   juice, and Juniper Simple Syrup together until well
   combined.

2. Add nonalcoholic aperitif to the shaker.

3. Add large cubes of ice, cover the shaker, and shake
   vigorously 10–12 seconds or until the exterior of the
   shaker becomes visibly frosty.

4. Place a big cube of ice in a rocks glass. Then, to
   achieve a smooth texture, use a fine-mesh strainer
   to double-strain the mixture into the glass.

5. Finally, garnish with strawberry slice.

Kumquat and Sage Spritz

Kumquats are a unique type of citrus fruit that can be eaten whole—yes, including the peel! This mocktail uses a few whole kumquats, making this a citrus-forward drink. Sage leaves are also used to infuse it with herbal notes that also elevate the bitterness of the nonalcoholic Italian red aperitif.

SERVES 1

Ingredients

4 whole kumquats

½ ounce Orange Simple Syrup (see recipe in Chapter 1)

4 sage leaves

2 ounces nonalcoholic Italian red aperitif

2 ounces tonic water

1 sage sprig for garnish

Mocktail Twist

Kumquats are small, oval-shaped citrus fruit native to Southeast Asia. Unique among citrus fruit, they can be eaten whole—skin, seeds, and all. Kumquats are not only cute, but also a good source of vitamin C and fiber. They are also believed to bring good fortune. In Chinese culture, kumquats are considered a symbol of good luck and prosperity.

1. In a cocktail shaker, add 4 kumquats and Orange Simple Syrup.

2. Using a muddler or the back of a wooden spoon, muddle the ingredients and extract all the juice out of the kumquat.

3. Add sage leaves and nonalcoholic aperitif to the shaker.

4. Add large cubes of ice, cover the shaker, and shake 10–12 seconds or until the exterior of the shaker becomes visibly frosty.

5. Using a fine-mesh strainer, double-strain the mixture into a rocks glass.

6. Top with tonic water and lightly stir. Carefully add a big cube of ice.

7. Garnish with sprig of sage.

General Giuseppe

This drink draws inspiration from the cocktail called the Garibaldi, a red-orange drink named after Italian General Giuseppe Garibaldi, who helped unify the nation of Italy. There are not many ingredients in this drink, which relies primarily on the freshness of the orange juice. A few dashes of orange bitters are also used to add a layer of depth.

SERVES 1

Ingredients

2 ounces nonalcoholic Italian red aperitif

4 ounces fresh orange juice

3 dashes alcohol-free orange bitters

1 orange wedge for garnish

Mocktail Twist

Using fresh-squeezed orange juice is key to this drink. Dry shaking the ingredients helps add texture to the drink. A frother can also be used to aerate the mixture prior to shaking it with ice. In Italy, the Garibaldi cocktail is often enjoyed during the aperitivo hour, a time where people gather before dinner to enjoy drinks and light snacks. Throw your own aperitivo hour in your backyard and serve this easy-to-make mocktail. It would go well with a charcuterie board!

1. In a cocktail shaker, combine nonalcoholic aperitif, juice, and bitters.

2. Without adding any ice, cover the shaker and dry shake 10 seconds. This aerates the drink, resulting in a smooth texture.

3. Next, add large cubes of ice, cover the shaker, then shake 10–12 seconds to chill the mixture.

4. Fill a highball glass $2/3$ full with ice cubes. Strain the mixture into the highball glass, and then garnish with orange wedge on the rim of the glass.

Citrus Aperitivo Spritz

This mocktail draws inspiration from the Paloma cocktail but uses a nonalcoholic Italian aperitif instead of tequila. The grapefruit soda adds texture, thanks to the carbonation, along with a touch of sweetness. This recipe is also very easy to make! You just build it right in the glass—no need to use any specialty tools.

SERVES 1

Ingredients

2 ounces nonalcoholic Italian orange aperitif

½ ounce lemon juice

6 ounces grapefruit soda

1 ounce club soda

1 grapefruit wedge for garnish

Mocktail Twist

Grapefruit sodas are usually sweet, so you can play with the ratio of grapefruit soda to club soda according to your preferred taste.

1. In a highball glass, combine nonalcoholic aperitif, lemon juice, grapefruit soda, and club soda.

2. Gently add crushed ice to fill the glass and lightly stir.

3. Finally, garnish with grapefruit wedge, and there you have a simple but delicious mocktail!

Italian Summer

This mocktail combines nonalcoholic Italian red aperitif with tropical flavors that are normally mixed with rum, creating an "Italy meets Polynesia" type of drink that is truly enjoyable and unique. Although these two traditions are quite different from each other, when done correctly, the flavors complement each other well, as the bitterness from the aperitif marries nicely with the sweet and sour flavors of tropical drinks.

SERVES 1

Ingredients

2 ounces nonalcoholic Italian red aperitif

1½ ounces pineapple juice

½ ounce lemon juice

¼ ounce Simple Syrup (see recipe in Chapter 1)

2 dashes alcohol-free orange bitters

2 pineapple fronds and 1 maraschino cherry for garnish

Mocktail Twist

Have you ever heard someone order an "Aperitiki"? The word is a mash-up of "aperitivo" and "tiki" that appeared on the scene when mixologists began combining bitter aperitifs with the tropical flavors of tiki cocktails. Mimic an authentic tiki drink by "floating" 1 ounce rum alternative on top of the mixture after it is poured in the glass!

1. In a cocktail shaker, combine nonalcoholic aperitif, pineapple juice, lemon juice, Simple Syrup, and bitters.

2. Add large cubes of ice, cover the shaker, and shake vigorously 10–12 seconds or until the exterior of the shaker becomes visibly frosty.

3. Place a big cube of ice in a rocks glass then strain the mixture into the glass.

4. Garnish with pineapple fronds and cherry.

Citrus Party

One unique and creative way to incorporate sweetness, fruitiness, texture, and complexity to mocktails is by using jams and spreads. This delightful beverage uses a couple of spoonfuls of fig orange spread combined with other citrus flavors. If you like the bitter citrus flavors of Italian aperitifs like Campari, you're going to love this mocktail!

SERVES 1

Ingredients

1½ ounces nonalcoholic Italian red aperitif

2 teaspoons fig orange spread

¾ ounce lemon juice

3 ounces grapefruit juice

1 lemon peel for garnish

Mocktail Twist

Adding a splash of club soda to the drink as the last step is a good variation of this recipe. It will maintain its flavor while adding an enjoyable hint of carbonation.

1. Place a martini glass in the freezer, ensuring it becomes chilled while you prepare the drink.

2. In a cocktail shaker, combine nonalcoholic aperitif, fig orange spread, lemon juice, and grapefruit juice.

3. Add large cubes of ice, cover the shaker, and shake vigorously 12–15 seconds or until the exterior of the shaker becomes visibly frosty.

4. Using a fine-mesh strainer, double-strain the mixture into the chilled martini glass. This step effectively filters out any fruit remnants and small ice fragments, resulting in a smooth and refined mocktail.

5. Finally, garnish with lemon peel.

Vanilla Orange Dream

This mocktail uses the classic flavor combination of orange and vanilla. The citrusy bitterness of the nonalcoholic Italian orange aperitif is balanced out by the vanilla syrup and tart lemon juice. A few dashes of orange bitters bind all these flavors together. Finally, the egg white adds richness to it, giving the drink a frothy and silky texture.

SERVES 1

Ingredients

2 ounces nonalcoholic Italian orange aperitif

1 ounce lemon juice

$1/2$ ounce vanilla syrup

3 dashes alcohol-free orange bitters

$3/4$ ounce egg white

1 lemon peel for garnish

Mocktail Twist

Simple syrup can substitute for vanilla syrup (in the same amount), if you also add a couple drops of alcohol-free vanilla extract.

1. Place a coupe glass in the freezer, allowing it to chill as you prepare the mocktail. You can also use a Nick and Nora glass or a martini glass.

2. In a cocktail shaker, combine nonalcoholic aperitif, lemon juice, vanilla syrup, and bitters.

3. Using a jigger, measure $3/4$ ounce egg white and add that to the shaker. (Depending on the size of the egg, including the entire egg white can produce too much foam, so it is best to measure the egg white each time.)

4. Without adding any ice, cover the shaker and dry shake vigorously 20 seconds.

5. Add large cubes of ice to the shaker and wet shake another 10 seconds.

6. Using a fine-mesh strainer, double-strain the mixture into the chilled coupe glass.

7. Express the oils from lemon peel over the drink by squeezing the pith side of the peel toward the top of the drink so the oils spray into it. This helps mask the scent of the egg white on the foam.

8. Finally, garnish with lemon peel.

Margherita Analcolica

This mocktail is inspired by a classic cocktail category called a Daisy. The Daisy is a style of cocktail that consists of a base spirit, citrus juice, a sweetener, and possibly a liqueur or other modifier. This nonalcoholic version uses a nonalcoholic Italian red aperitif as its base spirit, along with orange juice as the sweetening agent and lime juice as the souring agent.

SERVES 1

Ingredients

1 ounce sea salt for glass rim

2 lime wedges, divided (1 for glass rim and 1 for garnish)

2 ounces nonalcoholic Italian red aperitif

1½ ounces fresh orange juice

½ ounce lime juice

Mocktail Twist

The salt rim should not be skipped as the salt balances the sweetness of the nonalcoholic aperitif and orange juice. To get the best of both worlds, only rim half of the glass with salt so you have the option to sip it with or without salt.

1. Place salt on a small plate.

2. Wet half the rim of a rocks glass using 1 lime wedge.

3. Dip that wet part of the rim into salt. Set the rocks glass aside.

4. Combine nonalcoholic aperitif, orange juice, and lime juice in a cocktail shaker.

5. Add large cubes of ice, cover the shaker, and shake vigorously 10–12 seconds or until the exterior of the shaker becomes visibly frosty.

6. Add a few cubes of ice into the salt-rimmed rocks glass.

7. Strain the mixture into the glass.

8. Finally, garnish with 1 lime wedge on the rim of the glass.

CHAPTER 8

SPIRIT-FREE MOCKTAILS

Although the "dry industry" has created an impressive array of nonalcoholic options that can substitute for or mimic the taste of alcoholic spirits, these nonalcoholic spirits can be hard to find in some areas. Perhaps the dry movement just hasn't reached your community yet, or maybe you just used your last bottle of nonalcoholic spirit but still need to whip up an adult beverage with your friends. Don't worry, there are several delicious "spirit-free" alternatives that don't use an alcohol substitute.

This chapter contains recipes that use ingredients that are easy to find and still make your mocktails exciting. With some creativity, you can create drinks that are balanced, that are not too sweet, and that even pack a punch! Teas, ginger shots, dried berries, and shrubs are just a few ways to achieve complexity even without spirit alternatives. Most of these ingredients are also packed with nutrients!

Elderflower Cucumber Fizz

Juniper berries give gin its distinctive pine-like flavor and aroma.
In this drink, dried juniper berries are used in two ways: as an ingredient
in the Juniper Simple Syrup, and by muddling them with cucumbers. These
methods effectively infuse the drink with the botanical flavors of the
juniper berries, which complement the fresh, subtle vegetal taste of
cucumbers and the floral essence of elderflower.

SERVES 1

Ingredients

$1/4$ cup chopped unpeeled
cucumber

$1/2$ ounce lemon juice

1 ounce Juniper Simple Syrup
(see recipe in Chapter 1)

10 dried juniper berries

6 ounces elderflower tonic water

1 mint sprig and 1 cucumber
ribbon for garnish (see
instructions in Chapter 1)

Mocktail Twist

The versatile juniper berry has
been used in Native American
herbal medicine for its diuretic,
digestive, and antiseptic properties.
In culinary contexts, dried juniper
berries are used in marinades,
rubs, and sauces. And as
explained in this book, juniper
berries can be used to convincingly
mimic the flavor of gin.

1. In a cocktail shaker, combine chopped cucumber, lemon juice, Juniper Simple Syrup, and berries.

2. Using a muddler or the back of a wooden spoon, muddle cucumber and berries with the liquids, making sure to extract the juice out of the cucumber.

3. Add large cubes of ice, cover the shaker, and shake vigorously 10–12 seconds or until the exterior of the shaker becomes visibly frosty.

4. Fill a highball glass $2/3$ full with ice.

5. Using a fine-mesh strainer, double-strain the mixture into the glass. This step effectively filters out any remnants of the cucumber and berries.

6. Add tonic water then lightly stir.

7. Finally, garnish with mint sprig and a cucumber ribbon.

Passion Fruit Martini

Inspired by a provocatively named cocktail, the Porn Star Martini, this G-rated, spirit-free version balances out the tartness of the passion fruit and lime with the sweetness of the pineapple juice. To maintain some of the theatrical qualities of the original, however, this drink is served with a shot of nonalcoholic prosecco or sparkling apple juice, which can be either poured into the drink or taken separately as a shot before sipping this cheeky concoction.

SERVES 1

Ingredients

- 2 medium passion fruit, each cut in half
- 4 ounces pineapple juice
- $\frac{1}{2}$ ounce lime juice
- $\frac{1}{2}$ ounce vanilla syrup
- 1 shot sparkling apple juice or nonalcoholic prosecco

Mocktail Twist

According to CGA, a food and drink insight and research company, the Porn Star Martini was named the UK's favorite cocktail in the year 2018, beating the mojito and the Sex on the Beach.

1. Place a coupe glass in the freezer, allowing it to chill as you prepare the mocktail.
2. Scoop the seeds and flesh from 3 of the 4 passion fruit halves into a cocktail shaker. The remaining passion fruit half will be used for garnish later.
3. Add in pineapple juice, lime juice, and vanilla syrup.
4. Add large cubes of ice, cover the shaker, and shake vigorously 10–12 seconds or until the exterior of the shaker becomes visibly frosty.
5. To achieve a smooth texture, double-strain the mixture into the chilled coupe glass using a fine-mesh strainer, effectively removing any small ice fragments.
6. Garnish by floating the remaining half passion fruit on top of the drink.
7. Serve with sparkling apple juice or nonalcoholic prosecco in a shot glass.

Espresso and Tonic

This curious drink is perfect for those who like their coffee strong!
The chilled espresso provides bold and bitter flavors that go surprisingly well
with the slightly bitter and slightly citrusy flavors of tonic water. The texture
from the tonic water's carbonation is also a welcome addition!

SERVES 1

Ingredients

6 ounces tonic water

2 ounces chilled espresso

1 orange peel for garnish

Mocktail Twist

If you're looking for something
that's less bitter, you can replace
the espresso with the same
amount of cold brew concentrate
(available in most grocery
stores). Cold brew concentrates
are often smoother, lower in
acidity, and less bitter, although
some are also sweetened, so it
pays to be selective.

1. Fill a Collins glass $2/3$ full with ice cubes.

2. Gently pour in tonic water.

3. Top with chilled espresso.

4. Garnish with orange peel. You can also express the
   oil of the orange peel by squeezing the pith side of
   the peel toward the top of the drink so the oils spray
   over it if you'd like to make it citrusy.

Northern Lights

This mocktail takes its name from the stunning aurora borealis, or northern lights. The recipe uses a lemon and ginger shot with blue spirulina, which is available in many grocery stores or online. If lemon and ginger shots are not available in your area, the Ginger Shot recipe in Chapter 1 explains how to make your own shots from fresh ginger and lemons. Adding 1 teaspoon blue spirulina powder to that mix will give it the pop of blue color that makes this drink special.

SERVES 1

Ingredients

- 1 ounce nonalcoholic blue curaçao syrup
- 2 ounces lemon and ginger shot with blue spirulina
- 3 ounces butterfly pea flower tea (cooled to room temperature)
- 1/2 ounce lemon juice
- 1 lemon peel for garnish

Mocktail Twist

Butterfly pea flower tea is a caffeine-free herbal tea made from the flowers of a butterfly pea plant. Its taste is comparable to that of green tea.

1. Fill a highball glass 2/3 full with small ice balls or cubes.

2. Pour blue curaçao syrup into the glass and wait for it to settle at the bottom.

3. Next, carefully "layer in" ginger shot by placing the round end of a bar spoon directly over the ice and syrup in the glass, with the spoon's dome side up. Then decant (*slowly* pour) ginger shot over the domed end of the spoon, allowing ginger shot to trickle down the dome of the spoon as it gently settles on top of blue curaçao syrup without disturbing it. Ginger shot should remain separate from and float on top of blue curaçao syrup for a "layered" look.

4. Then use the same decanting technique to layer in tea on top of ginger shot.

5. Finally, pour lemon juice directly onto tea layer and watch its color change! Adding lemon juice or any acidic ingredient to the tea will transform its rich blue hue into a beautiful purple or pink shade.

6. Garnish with lemon peel on the rim of the glass.

7. Take a moment to admire its beauty (and show it off to your friends!) before stirring and enjoying.

Blueberry Mint Refresher

Made with fresh fruits and herbs, this drink is refreshingly delicious.
Muddling lime wedges incorporates tartness and a bit of bitterness, flavors which
are then balanced out by the sweetness of the blueberries. You can also replace the
blueberries with strawberries, or use basil leaves instead of mint leaves. Have fun!
And for a lower-calorie option, you can use a zero-sugar lemon-lime soda.

SERVES 1

Ingredients

$1/4$ cup blueberries

$3/4$ ounce Simple Syrup
(see recipe in Chapter 1)

2 lime wedges

$1/2$ ounce lime juice

6 mint leaves

$7 1/2$ ounces lemon-lime soda

3 blueberries, 1 lime wedge, and
1 mint sprig for garnish

Mocktail Twist

If the fine-mesh strainer gets clogged with blueberry pieces during the straining step, help the liquid through by teasing the blueberry pieces with a bar spoon or a regular spoon. This will release the liquid to flow through the strainer.

1. In a cocktail shaker, add $1/4$ cup blueberries and Simple Syrup.

2. Using a muddler or the back of a wooden spoon, muddle berries and syrup until well combined.

3. Add in 2 lime wedges and muddle some more.

4. Add lime juice and 6 mint leaves.

5. Add large cubes of ice, cover the shaker, and shake vigorously 10–12 seconds or until the exterior of the shaker becomes visibly frosty.

6. Fill a highball glass $2/3$ full with ice cubes.

7. Using a fine-mesh strainer, double-strain the mixture into the glass.

8. Top with lemon-lime soda.

9. To garnish, skewer 3 blueberries on a cocktail pick and then skewer on 1 lime wedge starting with the rind side. Place the garnish on the rim of the glass and add mint sprig on top of the drink.

Spiced Apple Ginger Mocktail

If you want an elevated drink with autumn flavors that still offers a kick, this recipe is for you. You will get a spicy kick from the Ginger Shot. The heat from the ginger is balanced out by the apple cider, which provides a good amount of sweetness. There's also a bit of cinnamon to add a touch of warmth to this fall-themed mocktail.

SERVES 1

Ingredients

½ ounce Ginger Shot (see recipe in Chapter 1)

5 ounces apple cider

⅛ teaspoon ground cinnamon

1 apple fan for garnish (see instructions in Chapter 1)

Mocktail Twist

If you like cinnamon, you can rim half of the glass with cinnamon sugar by first dipping the rim of the glass in simple syrup and then dipping the wet part in cinnamon sugar that you've spread out on a plate. This allows you to take in some pleasant cinnamon aroma before even tasting the mocktail.

1. Place a stemless martini glass in the freezer, allowing it to chill as you prepare the mocktail.

2. In a cocktail shaker, combine Ginger Shot, apple cider, and cinnamon.

3. Add large cubes of ice, cover the shaker, and shake vigorously 10–12 seconds or until the exterior of the shaker becomes visibly frosty.

4. Strain the mixture into the chilled stemless martini glass.

5. Garnish with apple fan.

B&T (Botanicals and Tonic)

This B&T (Botanicals and Tonic) is a good nonalcoholic substitute
to the classic G&T (Gin and Tonic), especially if you don't have access
to gin alternatives in your area. Juniper berries are real gin's signature
ingredient and you can buy dried juniper berries in most grocery
stores, usually in the spice aisle, or online.

SERVES 1

Ingredients

2 lime wedges

$\frac{1}{2}$ ounce lime juice

7 dried juniper berries

$7\frac{1}{2}$ ounces tonic water

1 lime peel for garnish

Mocktail Twist

Since most of this drink consists of tonic water, choose a good quality tonic water to ensure superior taste. There are Mediterranean tonic waters, premium Indian tonic waters, and even flavored options like elderflower tonic waters.

1. In a cocktail shaker, add lime wedges, lime juice, and berries.

2. Using a muddler or the back of a wooden spoon, muddle the ingredients together, lightly cracking the berries to release their flavors.

3. Add large cubes of ice, cover the shaker, and shake vigorously 10–12 seconds or until the exterior of the shaker becomes visibly frosty. Since there is not a lot of liquid in this recipe, shaking it will result in a beneficial amount of water being added to it. The water will also neutralize the tartness of the lime juice.

4. Fill a highball glass $\frac{2}{3}$ full with ice cubes.

5. Using a fine-mesh strainer, double-strain the mixture into the glass. Note that the volume of the yield is small—about an ounce of liquid from the lime juice and dilution—but this liquid is packed with flavors.

6. Top with tonic water.

7. Garnish with lime peel.

Lavender Lemon Bliss

Many beverages, oftentimes nonalcoholic ones, are infused with ashwagandha root extract. Ashwagandha is considered an adaptogen, which is said to help the body adapt to stress and reduce anxiety. This mocktail uses ashwagandha tea, which is available in some grocery stores or online. Its bitter flavors are balanced out by the floral sweetness from the Lavender Simple Syrup.

SERVES 1

Ingredients

3 ounces ashwagandha tea
(cooled to room temperature)

1½ ounces Lavender Simple
Syrup (see recipe in
Chapter 1)

2 ounces lemon juice

1 lavender sprig or 1 edible
flower for garnish

Mocktail Twist

To make the ashwagandha tea, steep 1 ashwagandha tea bag in 8 ounces boiling water for 5 minutes. Ashwagandha is bitter so you can adjust the taste by steeping the tea bag for a shorter time. Let tea cool to room temperature before using in the mocktail.

1. In a cocktail shaker, combine tea, Lavender Simple Syrup, and lemon juice.

2. Add large cubes of ice, cover the shaker, and shake vigorously 10–12 seconds or until the exterior of the shaker becomes visibly frosty.

3. Fill a double rocks glass $2/3$ full with ice.

4. Strain the mixture into the glass.

5. Finally, garnish with lavender sprig or edible flower.

Orange Ginger Bloom

Using teas in mocktails is a good way to add complexity to the drink without spirit alternatives. This mocktail uses hibiscus tea for both its strikingly beautiful color and for its potential health benefits. Hibiscus tea is believed to help maintain healthy cholesterol and blood pressure levels. When it comes to flavor, hibiscus tea gives this drink hints of berry and citrus.

SERVES 1

Ingredients

1 ounce ginger syrup

2 ounces fresh orange juice

4 ounces hibiscus tea (cooled to room temperature)

1 orange peel for garnish

Mocktail Twist

To make the hibiscus tea, steep 1 hibiscus tea bag in 6 ounces boiling water for 7 minutes. Let tea cool to room temperature before using in the mocktail.

1. Fill a highball glass $2/3$ full with small ice balls or cubes.

2. Pour in ginger syrup and wait for it to settle at the bottom of the glass.

3. Next, carefully "layer in" juice by placing the round end of a bar spoon directly over the ice and syrup in the glass, with the spoon's dome side up. Then decant (*slowly* pour) juice over the domed end of the spoon, allowing juice to trickle down the dome of the spoon as it gently settles on top of ginger syrup without disturbing it. Juice should remain separate from and float on top of ginger syrup for a "layered" look.

4. Then use the same decanting technique to layer in tea on top of juice.

5. The result is a tri-layered drink with ginger syrup at the bottom, followed by orange juice, and topped with hibiscus tea.

6. Finally, garnish with orange peel.

Berry Bush

"Shrubs" are flavored syrups that combine fruits, sugar, and vinegar, and they are a good way to add depth and complexity to nonalcoholic cocktails. Once you have the shrub made, all you need to do is add some carbonated water and you have an elevated mocktail. Once you've mastered the art of making shrubs, you can mix and match with different fruits and different kinds of vinegar.

SERVES 1

Ingredients

- $6\frac{1}{2}$ ounces elderflower tonic water
- $1\frac{1}{2}$ ounces Berry Shrub (see recipe in Chapter 1)
- 1 medium strawberry for garnish

Mocktail Twist

The word "shrub" comes from the Arabic word "sharab," which means "to drink." Shrubs are also called drinking vinegars or vinegar cordials, but "shrub" certainly sounds more appetizing.

1. Fill a highball glass $\frac{2}{3}$ full with small ice cubes.

2. Gently pour in tonic water, leaving room for the Berry Shrub.

3. Top with Berry Shrub.

4. To garnish, slice off top of strawberry to remove the green cap. Make a notch in the middle of the flat, sliced part so you can place strawberry on the rim of the glass at the notch with pointed end of strawberry facing up.

US/METRIC CONVERSION CHART

VOLUME CONVERSIONS	
US Volume Measure	**Metric Equivalent**
⅛ teaspoon	0.5 milliliter
¼ teaspoon	1 milliliter
½ teaspoon	2 milliliters
1 teaspoon	5 milliliters
½ tablespoon	7 milliliters
1 tablespoon (3 teaspoons)	15 milliliters
2 tablespoons (1 fluid ounce)	30 milliliters
¼ cup (4 tablespoons)	60 milliliters
⅓ cup	90 milliliters
½ cup (4 fluid ounces)	125 milliliters
⅔ cup	160 milliliters
¾ cup (6 fluid ounces)	180 milliliters
1 cup (16 tablespoons)	250 milliliters
1 pint (2 cups)	500 milliliters
1 quart (4 cups)	1 liter (about)

WEIGHT CONVERSIONS	
US Weight Measure	**Metric Equivalent**
½ ounce	15 grams
1 ounce	30 grams
2 ounces	60 grams
3 ounces	85 grams
¼ pound (4 ounces)	115 grams
½ pound (8 ounces)	225 grams
¾ pound (12 ounces)	340 grams
1 pound (16 ounces)	454 grams

INDEX

ABOUT THE AUTHOR

Derick Santiago is a mixologist based in Southern California. He is the creator of Mocktail Wiz, an *Instagram* page (@mocktailwiz) and website (MocktailWiz.com) dedicated to craft mocktails and mindful mixology techniques. He has worked as a mocktail recipe designer, photographer, and video creator with leading brands in the nonalcoholic beverage industry.